THE MATH
BEHIND
WALL STREET

THE MATH BEHIND WALL STREET

How the Market Works and How to Make It Work for You

by NICHOLAS TEEBAGY

Four Walls Eight Windows
New York/London

Published in the United States by:
Four Walls Eight Windows
39 West 14th Street, room 503
New York, N.Y., 10011

U.K. offices:
Four Walls Eight Windows/Turnaround
Unit 3, Olympia Trading Estate
Coburg Road, Wood Green
London N22 6TZ, England

Visit our website at http://www.fourwallseightwindows.com

First printing October 1998.

Library of Congress Cataloging-in-Publication Data:
Teebagy, Nicholas.
The math behind wall street: how the market works and how to make it work
for you/by Nicholas Teebagy.
p. cm.
ISBN 1-56858-111-4
1. Investments—Mathematics. I. Title.
HG4515.3.T44   1998
332.6′01′51—dc21
98-37942
CIP

10 9 8 7 6 5 4 3 2 1
Text design by PennSet, Inc.
Printed in the United States

To Joan, Christine and Andrea

CONTENTS

INTRODUCTION
By Amir D. Aczel

It is a pleasure for me to write the introduction to Dr. Nicholas Teebagy's book on the mathematics behind Wall Street. I believe that investors will benefit greatly from a book introducing them to the intricate mathematics that underlie the movements of the stock markets. Large investment companies have entire departments of quantitative analysts, "Quants," as they are called, working full-time to help the firm as a whole and individual investment advisors make better decisions. It is now time to give the average person access to the same tools the big players have in their arsenals as they tackle the uncertainty of investing in today's erratic asset markets.

October 19, 1987 was a landmark date in the history of Wall Street. Not since the stock market crash of 1929, which heralded the Great Depression, have the markets seen a drop in their values as they did that day in 1987. The big difference between the two events was in their respective aftermaths. For unlike the 1929 event, the one that occurred almost 60 years later was followed by a quick recovery of the markets, and with no immediate adverse consequences—except ones incurred by investors who panicked and sold their holdings. The event and the recovery have since taught us an important lesson about the Wall Street of the 1990s and beyond. The lesson is one about statistics.

The pre-1987 markets were more static than the ones that followed. Investments on Wall Street have provided Americans with the best long-term choice for growth of their hard-earned savings. Stocks on the Street have yielded an overall long-term return rate of over 10%, outpacing real estate, bonds, bank deposits, and other forms of investments for the buy-and-hold, long-term individual investor interested in keeping up with inflation, protecting the nest egg and enjoying additional profit. But most investors have no understanding of, or appreciation for, the immense power of risk.

As markets become more and more efficient and tiny bits of information can be interpreted quickly, resulting in vigorous reactions from investors, they become more dominated by *variance* than they have been in the past. It is no longer just the *average* long-term trend in yields that is the driving force behind investors' actions, but now the perception of risk—as captured by the statistical concept of variance—that plays a major driving force. The '87 crash illustrates this point. For the entire episode was a manifestation of the increasing variance of overall stock prices, which was to characterize the entire market of the following decade. While overall long-term market performance has improved in the 1990, giving investors tremendous advantages and opportunities, the variance of the markets has increased at least as dramatically.

The idea of variance and its effect on the markets becomes evident to anyone who follows the Street and remembers how things used to be in the not-so-distant past. Today, fluctuations of the Dow Jones average of over 100 points a day are not a rarity. This is in sharp contrast with past behavior of the markets, when a drop of 50 or even 30 points would make investors gasp and start worrying about the future of their investments. While the average return for stocks has gone up in the last few years, so has the variance in prices. The road ahead of us climbs steeply into alluring hefty returns on investment, but the road as also gotten more bumpy and now resembles a roller-coaster. Today's investors need the tools to help them understand the road ahead. They need a mathematical road map to the future.

The increase in the variance of stock market prices is only one of the phenomena encountered by the modern investor. The variance itself is a manifestation of the increasing sophistication of the investment community and its greater understanding of the fundamentals that drive today's markets. Not too long ago, an investor's main information source on the markets and the economy was the *Wall Street Journal* and a handful of similar publications. Since newspapers are published overnight, the flow of information to the investor came in packets separated by 24 hours each. What was printed in the paper was usually already acted upon by people who either already knew the information to be published the next day, or could anticipate it. Thus buying and selling pressure on the market was diffuse. Computers and the Internet have changed all that in a very dramatic way.

Globalization is changing the way we live and do business. World markets are becoming increasingly more efficient—and increasingly more complex. More than ever in our past, we need the quantitative tools necessary for making sound investment decisions.

In addition to business information—so crucial for making sound investing decisions—today's investor needs more. There is no substitute for understanding basic economic principles, the so-called "fundamentals" of the market. And nothing will replace diligent, in-depth scrutiny of earning statements and quarterly and annual reports of a company.

To try to learn where the market is heading, we would be wise to resort to mathematics. Since economic fundamentals have always been modelled by mathematical equations, and since equilibrium prices in efficient markets are defined by intersections of demand and supply curves, mathematics offers us an important starting point in our attempts to understand the forces that move the markets. In addition, the price of any asset sold in an efficient market is a speculative variable—it is given to the vagaries of market psychology, feelings, hunches, and information. The purchase of any stock or portfolio of securities is a crap shoot. This is especially true today with the increased variance inherent in the markets. In order to deal with the random variables of the market, we must make good use of the laws of probability and statistics. Statistics is the science of information, and it deals in concepts that have allowed scientists to gain a hold of uncertainty, understand it, and act accordingly. This is not to say that anyone can control the uncertainty. Recent efforts to suspend trading when the markets have been in sharp decline have all failed, since as soon as trading was resumed, the markets returned to the trend they were on before the suspension. Nicholas Teebagy aims to help you understand the basics of variability, trends, covariance, and beta, as well as other statistical concepts that impact the markets.

This book will introduce you to the idea of a *random variable*. All quantities affecting the market as well as the prices and rates of return of assets traded in efficient markets are random variables. It will also introduce you to the ideas of probability theory. How are probabilities assessed and used in determining the probable values of the variables involved in the markets? The discussion will help you understand the role of probabilities in assessing the *expected* return on a security or portfolio, as well as the *standard deviation* of returns—the quantity statisticians and financial analysts use as a proxy for risk.

Next comes the *covariance*, which accounts for the way two or more securities or portfolios move together within their risk bands. This important measure is used by all advanced financial analysts and quants. You will learn the meaning of covariance as a joint measure of the risk of several assets, and you will learn how to interpret the meaning of any value of the covariance. Using the covariance idea effectively can allow an investor to minimize portfolio risk while maintaining a high prespecified level of expected, or average, rate of return on the portfolio. In fact, the entire theory of portfolio management hinges on the important concept of covariance. Using covariance adeptly can even allow a shrewd investor to design a zero-risk portfolio by choosing to include in the portfolio assets whose correlation is negative. Such a "hedging" portfolio will exploit the negative correlations among various assets so that when one loses money on one asset, one immediately recovers the loss through the gain accruing from the other assets in the portfolio.

The idea of correlation and covariance leads inevitably to the immensely important concept of *beta*. First proposed in the 1960s as a measure of systematic risk within a portfolio, the beta is still the single most useful parameter used in financial analysis of risky assets traded in efficient markets. Beta measures the slope of the best-fitting line that explains the dependence of returns on an asset or portfolio on the entire stock market. As such, the beta is a measure of the systematic risk of an asset—a parameter that gives us an idea about how much risk can be diversified away. The beta is a sensitivity measure, which tells an investor how the security he or she is contemplating for inclusion in a portfolio depends on the stock market as a whole. Beta is also a measure of how risky an asset may be, as measured in an objective scale that compares the risk with the risk of the entire universe of stocks listed on the exchange. An aggressive, growth-oriented mutual fund, for example, will have a beta of two or more. A conservative, income-producing mutual fund whose managers aim for stability rather than quick above-market returns may have a beta of 0.8. Index funds typically will have a beta equal to one. By definition, such funds aim at mimicking the returns that would be offered by investing in the well-diversified market as a whole.

The concept of diversification to reduce risk hinges on optimal use of the information conveyed by the beta. A modern investor must be proficient in the nuances of the theory of risk and diversification if he or she is to make sound decisions that will produce an investment portfolio that will match its risk-return properties with the aspirations and attitudes towards risk of the individual owning the portfolio. Mathematics are an essential element in this theory and the beta is a powerful mathematical tool to be used by every prudent investor.

Today's markets offer much more than investments in stocks or bonds. The last few years have seen a veritable explosion in the number of investment instruments available to the investing public. An important component of the market are derived securities, or simply derivatives. Futures contracts to purchase or sell stock are traded, themselves, on the market. Here, the mathematics determining the valuation of these complex instruments is an absolute essential for anyone who dares enter these risky markets. There is no shortage of examples of investors—some of them organizations rather than individuals—which have fallen prey to their own desire for a quick profit without being armed with an understanding of the process followed by derived securities. The mathematics underlying derived securities is so hairy that even many competent mathematicians are uncertain about the details, and the specifics for this aspect of the market will have to be left to a later book.

The Math Behind Wall Street should prepare you for understanding the important concepts of mathematics, risk and return, basic statistical techniques, and economic ideas that are crucial for understanding how today's complex markets work. Enjoy!

ACKNOWLEDGMENTS

I wish to thank the following people who provided helpful suggestions and comments: Wu Dong, Norm Josephy, Barbara Nevils, John Saber, Erl Sorensen, Jay Sultan, Alex Zampieron. My thanks also goes to my editor and publisher John Oakes and the staff at Four Walls Eight Windows for invaluable assistance.

Finally, I wish to thank my wife Joan for her input and many suggestions, and especially for her support and encouragement.

1

PROBABILITY
AND RISK

Virtually all investment decisions concerning the stock market are based on future events. If we could foretell the future with certainty, investment decisions would be obvious. Clearly, this is not the case. We are forced to make decisions in the face of uncertainty. Probability models give us a way to deal with uncertainty in investment analysis.

A *probability* is a quantitative measure of uncertainty. The probability may be objective, as in games of chance. If you're betting on the flip of a coin, the probability of tossing the coin and getting heads is 0.50. In these cases, the probability can be thought of as the relative frequency of the event. If we toss the coin one hundred times, we expect heads about fifty times, or 50% of the flips. On the other hand, subjective probability involves personal judgment, information and intuition. An expert assessing the probability of a merger is making a personal judgment based on what he or she knows and feels about the situation. Most probability assessments in security analysis are subjective in nature. For example, consider an analyst who computes a probability assessment that "IBM stock will go up next week" based on mathematical models which use past information and relationships. This could still be considered a subjective probability, since it assumes the analyst's belief that the future will behave like the past in this situation. However, whether subjective or objective probabilities are involved, the same set of statistical measures and concepts holds.

There are several properties and laws that probabilities follow. Probabilities must be between 0 and 1. Zero implies the event cannot occur and 1 implies the event will definitely occur. If an event is as likely to occur as not occur, the probability of the event occurring is .50. In everyday conversation, we often describe probability in less formal terms. For example, people sometimes talk about "odds." If the odds are 1 to 1, the probability is $1/(1+1)$ or $\frac{1}{2}$; if the odds are 1 to 2, the probability is $1/(1+2)$ or $\frac{1}{3}$; and so on. Also, people sometimes say, "The probability is eighty percent." Mathematically, this probability is .80.

RANDOM VARIABLES

Future returns on a stock investment are uncertain. If probabilities can be assigned to all the possible return outcomes, then the return is an example of a *random variable*. There are many quantities in securities analysis which may be thought of as random variables. Some examples include future earnings per share and the future price of a security. A random variable is simply a variable that takes on numerical values, determined by chance. The assignment of probabilities to the different possible values of the random variable is conveyed by what is called the *probability distribution* of the random variable. These variables may be either discrete or continuous. A discrete variable can assume at most a countable number of values, whereas a continuous variable may take on any value in an interval of numbers. For now, we will only consider returns which are discrete. Later in this chapter we will discuss the best-known continuous distribution, the normal distribution.

Consider the Widget Company, a hypothetical company. We wish to forecast the rate of return for its stock over the next year. This return can be thought of as a random variable, because of the uncertainty involved. Based on the likelihood of certain events occurring, we may formulate a probability distribution for this rate of return. The actual probabilities may be derived from our own beliefs, a financial analyst's assessments, some mathematical model, or other information. The following table is a display of a probability distribution.

Probability Distribution for the Widget Co.

X = rate of return	P(X) = probability of X
2%	.20
6%	.50
10%	.30
	1.00

We considered only three possible return outcomes, 2%, 6% or 10% with probabilities .20, .50 and .30 respectively. A graph, as in Figure 1.1, is often a good way to view the distribution.

Figure 1.1   Graph of Probability Distribution
for the Widget Co.

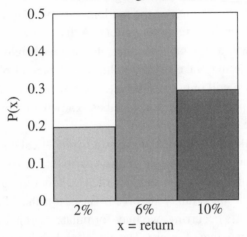

The events (or in this case the returns) of a probability distribution represent a list of outcomes which are mutually exclusive and collectively exhaustive. This means only one of the listed events must take place. Therefore, the sum of the probabilities will always equal 1.

EXPECTED VALUE

An investor would find it difficult to compare several different investment opportunities simply by looking at their probability distributions. One needs to compare the size of all the returns, along with their probabilities. Therefore a single number which summarizes the distribution—while it measures a particular characteristic of that distribution—is useful. These summary measures give the investor a better understanding of an investment and allow investment opportunities to be easily compared.

The *central tendency* is the most intuitive characteristic of the distribution. The *expected value* or *mean* is the most common measure of central tendency. It is computed by taking the weighted average of the different outcomes of the random variable where the weights are the probabilities. One interpretation of the expected value is a long run average. If many outcomes of the random variable can be observed, we would "expect" the average of these outcomes to be approximately equal to the expected value. The Greek letter μ is often used to represent the expected value. The formula for the expected value of a random variable, X, is given by:

$$E(x) = \mu = \sum_{all\,x} x\,P(x),$$

where the notation $\sum_{all\,x}$ means to sum for all values of X.

To demonstrate how this formula works, let's compute the "expected return" for the Widget Company's stock, using the probability distribution in the previous table:

$$E(x) = 2\%(.20) + 6\%(.50) + 10\%(.30) = 6.4\%$$

How do we explain the meaning of this 6.4%? One way is to say that if we were to make many investments whose returns have probability distributions similar to the Widget Co., then we would "expect" the average return to be approximately 6.4%.

Other measures of central tendency include the *mode* and *median*. The mode is the value that is most likely to occur. The median is the value where the random variable is equally likely to occur above it as below it. In this case, the mean is just another name for the expected value. To clarify the difference between these three measures, we'll compute each one using a simple data set that contains five returns. (This data set is the same as a probability distribution where all the values are equally likely.)

returns (%): 5, 10, 15, 20, 20

mode = 20   (most frequent value)

median = 15   (two values are above and two are below)

mean = (5+10+15+20+20)/5 = 14 (average value)

Returns which are extremely far from the center are called *outliers*. They are very different from the majority of returns in the distribution. If we wish a measure that is not sensitive to these outliers then the median is sometimes preferred over the mean. The mean is sensitive to these extreme values. Whereas the median only is affected if a value is above or below it and is not affected by its size. For example, suppose we change the last return of 20 in the previous data set to a return of 50. This 50 could be considered an outlier. The median does not change, but the mean increases to 20. The mean is sensitive to this extreme value of 50, whereas the median was not affected.

Figure 1.2 shows how the mean, median and mode compare for differently shaped distributions.

Figure 1.2 [A] is an example of a symmetrical distribution. In this case one half of the distribution is a mirror image of the other half and so the mean and median will be equal. If it is symmetrical with only one peak, then the mode will also be equal to the mean and median. Next is Figure 1.2[B], a right-skewed distribution. Here the mean is greater than the median. This will occur if the distribution of returns has a few extremely large values. The mean is sensitive to these extreme values, but the median is not. Finally, Figure 1.2[C] is an example of a left-skewed distribution. In this case, the mean will be less than the

Figure 1.2   Various Shaped Distributions of Returns

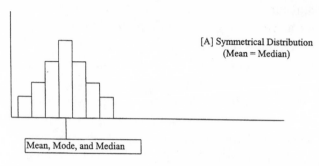

[A] Symmetrical Distribution
(Mean = Median)

Mean, Mode, and Median

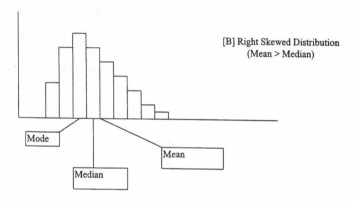

[B] Right Skewed Distribution
(Mean > Median)

Mode

Mean

Median

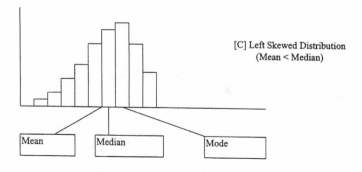

[C] Left Skewed Distribution
(Mean < Median)

Mean

Median

Mode

median. Here we are likely to have a few extremely low values.

Although any one of these three measures can be used to describe a distribution, the mean is preferred in securities analysis. One reason is that all information, both the values and their associated probabilities, of the random variable are used in the computation of the mean. If any one of these quantities is revised, the mean will almost always change, thus reflecting this revision. Another advantage to the mean is for portfolio analysis, where we will be interested in combining the central tendency measure of several securities into one portfolio measure. This can easily be done for the mean or expected value, but can not be done so easily for the median or the mode.

The expected value, however useful, does not provide all the information about a particular security. For example, suppose we are considering two investments, A and B. The following table displays the probability distributions for their rates of return for the next year.

Probability Distributions for the
Returns of Investments A and B

Investment A		Investment B	
return	P(return)	return	P(return)
–10%	.10	5%	.60
10%	.90	10%	.40

Which is the better investment? Computing the expected return for each, we get:

Expected (return for A) = –10%(.10) + (10%)(.90) = 8%
Expected (return for B) =   5%(.60) + (10%)(.40) = 7%

If we use the expected value as our only criteria, Investment A seems to be the better choice. But notice that an investment in A may lose money, whereas an investment in B will surely have a positive return. What is not reflected in the expected value is the risk of each investment. If we can not afford a loss of 10% on our investment, then B is our better choice. A prudent investor should be aware of and take into account the *risk* of any investment. In this example, with only two possible outcomes for each investment, it is easy to compare the risk. But what happens if there are many possible outcomes? We need a summary measure which will quantify the risk. One such measure is the standard deviation.

STANDARD DEVIATION AND VARIANCE

Variability, another characteristic of a distribution, can be measured several ways. The most popular method is the *standard deviation*. To compute the standard deviation, we must first compute the *variance*. The Greek letter σ is commonly used to represent the standard deviation and σ^2 the variance. The formulas for these quantities are given below.

$$\text{Variance} = \sigma^2 = \sum_{all\, x} (x-\mu)^2 P(x)$$
$$\text{Standard Deviation} = \sigma = \sqrt{\sigma^2}$$

The variance is computed by first squaring the deviation of each outcome from the mean or expected outcome. Then, a weighted average of these squared deviations is taken where, like the expected value, the weights are the corresponding probabilities of the outcomes. Finally, the standard deviation is computed by taking the square root of the variance, which returns the measure to the original units of the random variable.

It is useful to see how the variance is computed in order to gain a full understanding of how it measures dispersion. The variance and standard deviation for the rate of return of the Widget Co. follows:

variance $= \sigma^2 = (2-6.4)^2\,(.20) + (6-6.4)^2\,(.50) + (10-6.4)^2\,(.30) = 7.84$
standard deviation $= \sigma = \sqrt{7.84} = 2.8\%$

As our example shows, the standard deviation is a summary quantity that measures how far the actual returns of 2%, 6%, and 10% lie from the expected return of 6.4%. Thus, if the possible returns are closer to the expected return, the standard deviation is smaller, reflecting a smaller risk. Since the variance and standard deviation measure how much the actual returns deviate from the expected return, it is often used as a measure of the risk of an investment. To see how this can be used to compare investments, recall the probability distributions for Investments A and B from the last section. Computing the standard deviation for A we get 6.0% and for B we get 2.4%. Not surprisingly, the standard deviation is higher for A, which exhibits a greater amount of risk.

THE NORMAL DISTRIBUTION

Consider, again, the rate of return for the Widget Co.'s stock. Previously, we used Figure 1.1 to describe the probability distribution. In order to better understand the concept of a continuous distribution such as the normal distribution, the probability of each value is associated with the area of the rectangle over that value. A more realistic model than that of Figure 1.1 may be one in which there are more than three possible events,

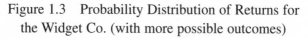

Figure 1.3 Probability Distribution of Returns for
the Widget Co. (with more possible outcomes)

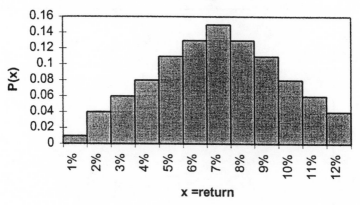

since usually the return may take on many different possible values. In Figure 1.3, there are twelve possible outcomes.

Notice that the probability of each value is less, and the rectangles have become thinner. If we continue defining the return in finer and finer detail, ultimately we have a continuous random variable, where the return may be any value in a given interval. The most popular continuous distribution is the *normal distribution* (Figure 1.4).

The height of the curve no longer represents the probability of a particular value, since the rectangles have become so thin they no longer have any width. The probability of any specific value is zero, since probabilities are now measured as areas under the curve. For example, the probability that a return takes on a value between 5% and 12% is the area under the curve, f(x), between the points x = 5% and x = 12%, see Figure 1.5.

The function f(x) is called the *probability density function* of the continuous random variable x. Note that the total area un-

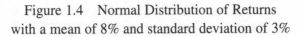

Figure 1.4   Normal Distribution of Returns
with a mean of 8% and standard deviation of 3%

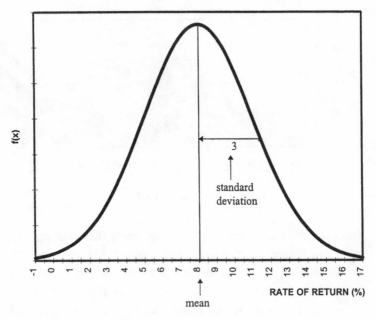

der the curve must always equal one, since it represents the total probability.

Figure 1.4 is the bell-shaped or normal distribution. It is the most widely used continuous distribution. If a value is affected by many different random disturbances, then the normal distribution may be a good approximation to its distribution. For example, since a future stock price is affected by many uncertain events, the normal is often successfully used to model its distribution.

Two parameters characterize a normal distribution: the mean, μ, and the standard deviation, σ. There are an infinite

Figure 1.5   The Area Under the Normal Curve
Represents Probability

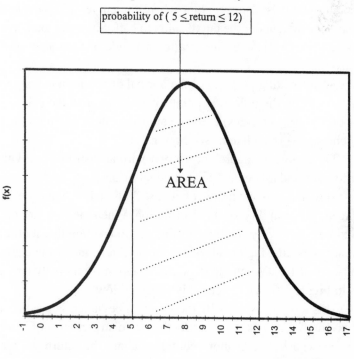

number of possible normal distributions, depending on the value of the mean and the value of the standard deviation. The basic shape of all normal distributions is always the same: a symmetric mound shape. Knowing the mean and the standard deviation (or equivalently, the variance) fixes a particular normal random variable out of the infinite collection of such variables. As noted earlier, the mean of the distribution is a measure of location. It tells us where the center of the distribution lies.

Since the normal distribution is symmetrical with one peak, the mean is also the mode and the median of the probability distribution; thus it is also the point where the curve is highest and where the area under the curve splits in half. Since the total area under the curve is one, the area to each side of the mean must equal 0.5.

An interesting property of the normal distribution is that the distance from the inflection point (that point where the concavity of the curve changes) to the mean (the center line) to is equal to one standard deviation (see Figure 1.4).

The following figure shows two normal distributions with different standard deviations, but equal means.

The standard deviation of a distribution is a measure of spread, or variability, of the distribution. When the standard deviation is relatively small, as in Figure 1.6 (A), the distribution is narrow with a high peak (since the total area under the curve must equal 1.0). When the standard deviation is relatively large, as in Figure 1.6 (B), the curve is wide and low.

This re-emphasizes why the standard deviation is used as a measure of total risk. Comparing the two distributions in Figure 1.6, we can be much more confident about the return we are likely to receive if our investment follows the distribution of (A) rather than (B). In (A) we are more likely to receive a return close to the mean of 8%, whereas in (B) the return could be far from the mean.

Figure 1.6   Normal Distributions for Rates of Returns With
Equal Means But Different Standard Deviations

(A) Standard Deviation Equal to 1.0

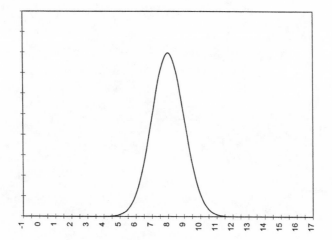

(B) Standard Deviation Equal to 3.0

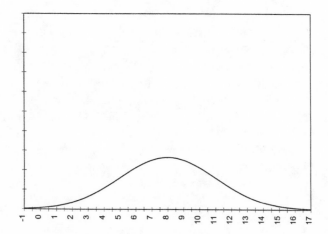

2

MODERN PORTFOLIO THEORY

A *portfolio* is a collection of securities owned by an investor. It may contain a variety of investments such as stocks, bonds, or treasury bills. How do we characterize the future returns and measure the risk of a portfolio? In the last chapter we discussed how we calculate and interpret key measures that describe the future returns for an individual security. We saw how the expected value measured the average of all the possible future returns and the standard deviation can be used as a measure of risk. Similarly, we will calculate the same measures for a portfolio. The calculation for the expected return is straightforward, but the calculation for the standard deviation will involve the covariance, a statistical measure that quantifies the relationship between the returns of two different securities. The covariance is an important concept for an investor to understand, since it is a crucial component in determining the risk of a portfolio.

A basic objective in the selection of securities for a portfolio is diversification. By diversifying an investor can reduce the total risk of his or her portfolio. In the 1950s, Harry Markowitz, a Nobel Prize winner, developed the portfolio model that quantifies the portfolio diversification process. He formalized the intuitive concepts of return and risk into the theory of the mean-variance analysis for a portfolio.

EXPECTED RETURN FOR A PORTFOLIO

A portfolio is a collection of numerous securities. Since each security's future return may be thought of as a random variable, the future return of a portfolio can also be thought of as a random variable. As with individual securities, the expected return for a portfolio provides the investor with a quantity that represents the average of all the possible future returns for that particular portfolio.

The expected return for a portfolio, not surprisingly, is dependent on the expected returns of the individual securities that make up the portfolio. The proportion of the portfolio's total value that each security represents is also needed. This proportion is the relative weight of each security. To compute the expected return of the portfolio, we calculate a weighted average of the expected returns of the individual securities. The formula is given below:

$$\mu_p = \sum_{all\ x} W_i \mu_i.$$

Where μ_p = the expected return of the portfolio,
           μ_i = the expected return of security i,
           W_i = the relative weight of security i,
and $\sum_{all\ i}$ means to sum over all the values of i

The following example illustrates how to apply this formula. Consider a portfolio that contains the three securities: S1, S2 and S3. The present value in each of the three is $3,000, $5,000, and $2,000, respectively. Using this information, we compute the relative weights.

Computations for the Relative Weights

Security	Present Value	Relative Weight, W_i
S1	$3,000	$3,000/$10,000 = .30
S2	$5,000	$5,000/$10,000 = .50
S3	$2,000	$2,000/$10,000 = .20
Total	$10,000	1.00

Suppose the estimated expected rate of return for each of the three stocks is 6%, 10%, and 8%, respectively. This information, along with the necessary calculations for computing the expected return, are displayed in in the following table.

Computations for the Expected Return for a Portfolio

Security	Relative Weight, W_i	Expected Return, μ_i	$W_i \times \mu_i$
S1	.30	6%	.30 x 6% = 1.8%
S2	.50	10%	.50 x 10% = 5.0%
S3	.20	8%	.20 x 8% = 1.6%
			$\mu_p = 8.4\%$

The expected rate of return for this portfolio is 8.4%.

COVARIANCE AND CORRELATION

Of concern to an investor is the risk associated with a particular portfolio and ways in which this risk can be reduced. One way to reduce risk is diversification. For example, suppose we are considering several different stocks for our portfolio, where prices will increase or decrease depending on the weather. Stock S's price will increase on sunny days, otherwise it will decrease in value. Conversely, Stock C's price will increase on cloudy days and decrease on sunny days. If we then only bought Stock S for our portfolio and we had a period of cloudy weather, our portfolio would perform very poorly. On the other hand, if we purchased a mixture of Stock S and C, then the portfolio's performance would not do so poorly in cloudy weather. Similarly, if we only bought stock C, then during sunny periods our portfolio would do very poorly. By purchasing a mixture of stocks S and C, we guard against significant losses no matter what the weather. Conversely, by purchasing this mixture we prevent ourselves from making significantly high gains. This is the result of reducing risk. It is to reduce the variability of future returns.

Purchasing securities that move up and down together would not have reduced our risk. For example, if we purchased many different stocks, but they all increased only on sunny days, it would not help our portfolio on the cloudy days. Therefore, the crucial step in diversifying is to select securities which do not move closely together, and ideally are inversely related. It is important to determine how securities are related to each other and ideally to be able to quantify their relationship. The covariance and correlation are measures that help do this. These measures are important and used considerably in the analysis of stock market data. Measuring the risk of a portfolio is just one application.

Covariance is a statistical quantity which measures the (linear) relationship between two variables. In our case, we will use the covariance to quantify the relationship between the returns for two securities. A large positive covariance implies that the returns move together. That is, if one security's return is high then the other security's return will also tend to be high. On the other hand, if the security has a low return, then the other will also tend to be low. Figure 2.1 displays a scatter plot for two securities with a high positive covariance. In this type of plot the returns for one security are plotted on the horizontal axis, while the returns for the other are plotted along the vertical axis.

Figure 2.1   Returns with Positive Covariance

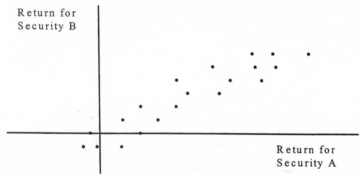

If two securities have a large negative covariance, then the returns tend to move in opposite directions. This is demonstrated in Figure 2.2 . Here we see that if one security's return is high then the other tends to be low.

Finally, if two securities have a very weak linear relationship, then the covariance would be approximately zero. An ex-

Figure 2.2 Returns with Negative Covariance

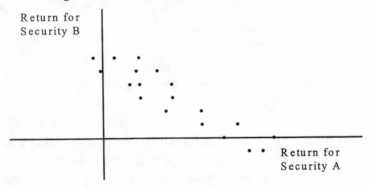

ample of this is shown in Figure 2.3. Here we see that there is no clear trend in the scatter of points. When one security is high the other may or may not be high.

Figure 2.3 Returns with Zero Covariance

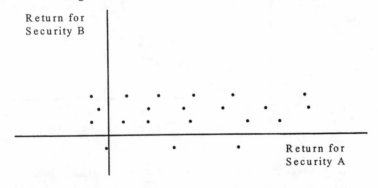

How does the covariance actually measure this relationship between the two variables? X_i represents the return for one security and X_j represents the return of the other security. Mathematically the covariance is defined to be:

$$\sigma_{ij} = \text{expected value of } [(X_i - \mu_i)(X_j - \mu_j)]$$

where σ_{ij} = the covariance between securities X_i and X_j,

μ_i = expected return for security i,

and, μ_j = expected return for security j.

(see endnote[i])

What values are generated by the key quantity $[(X_i - \mu_i)(X_j - \mu_j)]$? This is best seen in Figure 2.4. Here we see that the quantity will be positive in two cases. One, when returns X_i and X_j are both above their respective means and two, when both are below their respective means. Therefore, the covariance will be a sum of mostly positive values if the returns tend to move together. In other words, if one return tends to be high, then the other also tends to be high. When one is low, the other tends to also be low. This is the case we previously saw in Figure 2.1.

The quantity $[(x_i - \mu_i)(x_j - \mu_j)]$ will be negative when one of the returns is above its mean while at the same time the other is below its mean. Therefore, the covariance will be a sum of mostly negative values if the returns tend to move in an opposite direction, that is if one return tends to be high while the other tends to be low (Figure 2.2).

Finally, if there is no clear trend in the relationship between the two returns, then when one security's return is high the other may be high or low. In this case, the covariance will be a sum of both positive and negative values, resulting in a value close to zero. Figure 2.3 was an example of this case.

We know that the stronger the linear relationship, the further the covariance is away from zero, and the larger it is either in the positive direction or negative direction. But how large is large? Given a computed value of the covariance, it is difficult to determine if it represents a high value or not. This is where

Figure 2.4   Sign of $[(x_i - \mu_i)(x_j - \mu_j)]$

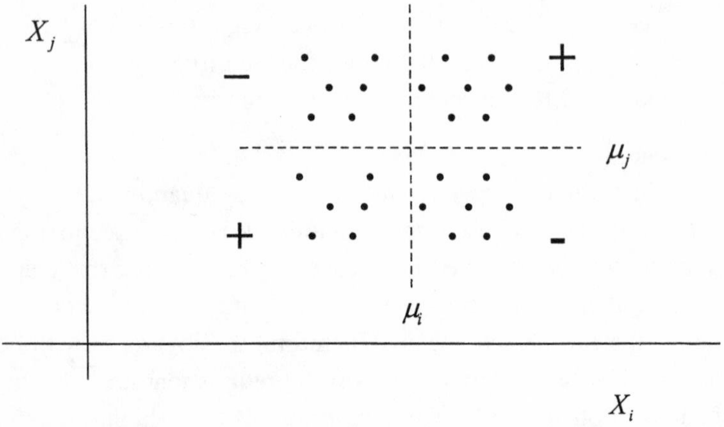

the correlation is useful. The *correlation* is computed by dividing the covariance by the standard deviations of the two securities. The formula is given by

$$\rho_{ij} = \frac{\sigma_{ij}}{\sigma_i \sigma_j}$$

where σ_{ij} = the covariance of security i and j
           σ_i = the standard deviation for security i,
           σ_j = the standard deviation for security j,
and ρ_{ij} = the correlation between securities i and j.

The sign of the correlation always has the same sign as the covariance, since the standard deviations must always be positive. So everything we discussed earlier concerning the sign of the covariance applies to the sign of the correlation.

The correlation formula divides the covariance by the standard deviations of the two securities. This has the effect of standardizing the covariance and thereby forcing the value of the correlation to be between −1 and +1. A value of −1 would be a perfect negative linear relationship and a +1 would be a perfect positive relationship. A perfect relationship between two securities would imply that the one return can be exactly determined by knowing the other security's return. Since this is rarely if ever the case, the −1 and +1 can be thought of as simply the boundary points for the correlation, where the closer the correlation is to −1 or +1 the stronger the relationship.

Recall that the weaker the relationship between the two securities' returns the closer the covariance will be to zero. Now notice that the closer the covariance is to zero the closer the correlation will be to zero. Therefore, as is the case for the covariance, the closer the correlation is to zero the weaker is the relationship between the two securities. Also notice that in the extreme case, when there is absolutely no linear relationship and the covariance is zero, the correlation will also be zero.

It should be easy to see why the covariance, and so the correlation, are important quantities when analyzing the risk of a portfolio. Consider our earlier example concerning Stock S, the stock that does well on sunny days, and Stock C, the stock that does well on cloudy days. The covariance between the stocks' returns would be a large negative number, and so the correlation would be close to -1. Therefore, intuitively we see that stocks with negative covariance would greatly reduce the risk of a portfolio, whereas stocks with large positive covariance would not be as helpful in reducing the risk. This is precisely what we will see mathematically when we discuss how to compute the standard deviation and consequently the risk of a portfolio.

VARIANCE AND STANDARD DEVIATION FOR A PORTFOLIO

Similarly to an individual security, the total risk of a portfolio can be measured by computing its variance and standard deviation. The general formula for the variance of a portfolio is given by:

$$\text{variance} = \sigma_p^2 = \sum_{all\ i}\sum_{all\ j} W_i W_j \sigma_{ij}.$$

Recall that W_i is the relative weight of security i and σ_{ij} is the covariance between securities i and j. The standard deviation, as always, is the square root of the variance.[1]

In order to better understand this equation, let's write it for the case where there are only two securities in the portfolio. Then the variance becomes:

$$\sigma_p^2 = W_1 W_1 \sigma_{11} + W_1 W_2 \sigma_{12} + W_2 W_1 \sigma_{21} + W_2 W_2 \sigma_{22}$$

Since σ_{11} is the covariance of security 1's return with itself, it is equal to the variance. Thus σ_{11} equals σ_1^2 and similarly σ_{22} equals σ_2^2. Further, since the covariance of returns i and j is equal to the covariance j and i, then σ_{12} equals σ_{21}. So the variance formula for two securities simplifies to:

$$\sigma_p^2 = W_1^2 \sigma_1^2 + W_2^2 \sigma_2^2 + 2 W_1 W_2 \sigma_{12}$$

To compute the variance of a portfolio first sum the variances of the individual securities, each multiplied by the square of their respective relative weights. Then add to this sum the covariances, where each is multiplied by the relative weights of the corresponding securities.

---

[1] standard deviation = $\sigma_p = \sqrt{\sum_{all\ i}\sum_{all\ j} W_i W_j \sigma_{ij}}$

Mathematically, this shows that the higher the covariance, in the positive direction (and all other things being equal), the greater the risk of a portfolio. The risk is thus reduced by choosing securities with a small covariance. Ideally, we would want to choose securities which have a negative covariance or correlation. Let's use our extreme case of the "cloudy" and "sunny" stocks as an example. Suppose the correlation is equal -1. This implies that the covariance equals $\sigma_{ij} = (-1.0)\sigma_i\sigma_j$. (Recall that the correlation $= \rho_{ij} = \frac{\sigma_{ij}}{\sigma_i\sigma_j}$.)

Now suppose we invest according to the weights $W_1 = \frac{\sigma_2}{\sigma_1+\sigma_2}$ and $W_2 = \frac{\sigma_1}{\sigma_1+\sigma_2}$. Using the equation for the variance of a portfolio containing two securities, what would the variance of this portfolio equal?

$$\sigma_p^2 = \left(\frac{\sigma_2}{\sigma_1+\sigma_2}\right)^2\sigma_1^2 + \left(\frac{\sigma_1}{\sigma_1+\sigma_2}\right)^2\sigma_2^2 + 2\left(\frac{\sigma_2}{\sigma_1+\sigma_2}\right)\left(\frac{\sigma_1}{\sigma_1+\sigma_2}\right)(-1.0)\sigma_1\sigma_2 = 0$$

So the variance is equal to 0 or no risk, exactly what we argued before. Thus, the mathematics is consistent with our intuition. Selecting stocks with low or negative correlation will help reduce the risk of a portfolio. Notice that in this extreme case we have constructed a risk free portfolio from two risky securities. The key that made this possible was the perfect negative correlation between the two stocks, which rarely, if ever, would occur in practice.

PORTFOLIO SELECTION

An investor is faced with the problem of deciding what mixture of securities make up the optimal portfolio. In making the decision between two possible portfolios, the investor must consider the return versus the risk of each portfolio. The expected return and standard deviation are used to help guide the investor during this decision making process. Most investors are risk-averse. This means that given two portfolios which have the same expected return, most investors would select the one with the smaller risk or standard deviation. The desire is to achieve the highest possible expected return while bearing an acceptable risk. Thus, one objective in portfolio selection is to diversify so as to obtain a low standard deviation, while at the same time achieving the highest possible expected return. The purpose of diversifying is to reduce the variability of returns. Finally, there are usually trade-offs between expected return and risk. Each individual investor must consider his or her own risk tolerance when making investment decisions.

Markowitz, the architect of modern portfolio theory, developed a portfolio selection model based on the expected returns and standard deviations of the candidate portfolios. The first step in this procedure is to derive the feasible set of all risky portfolios. This is the set all possible portfolios that can be derived from the group of available risky securities. The efficient set or frontier is then obtained by selecting the portfolios from the feasible set based on a risk averse criteria. That is, for a given standard deviation, the portfolio with the highest expected return becomes part of the efficient set. This is done for each possible standard deviation. This is demonstrated in the following figure, where the expected return is plotted along the vertical axis and the standard deviation is plotted along the horizontal axis.

The scatter points represent the feasible set and the efficient frontier is all the points on the arc from B to C. Any portfolio located on the arc BC has a higher expected return than any other portfolio of the same standard deviation. An investor

Figure 2.5 Feasible Set and Efficient Frontier

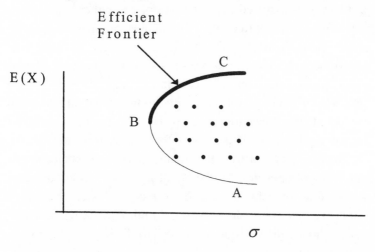

should only consider portfolios in the efficient frontier. The portfolio located at point B is the absolute minimum variance portfolio. No other portfolio has a smaller variance or standard deviation.

In order to find the efficient frontier, an advanced mathematical procedure called quadratic programming is used. The inputs to the procedure are the expected returns, standard deviations and covariances of the individual securities. It then solves for the weights of each security in the portfolio.

At this point, once the efficient frontier is found, the investor must decide which portfolio is best, dependent on the risk-return trade-off. Based on risk preference and without the inclusion of any risk free lending or borrowing, one of the portfolios lying on the efficient frontier would be optimal.

The next step is to consider what happens if we introduce

risk-free lending and borrowing into the portfolio selection problem. It is assumed that the investor can either lend or borrow money at a risk free rate. For example, an investor can purchase Treasury Bills. These are guaranteed by the U.S. government and the rate of return is known at the time of purchase. A risk-free asset has a certain pre-determined rate of return. So, the expected return is equal to the actual rate of return and the standard deviation is zero. Usually, the rates given by Treasury Bills are used as a proxy for the risk-free rate.

Now we will construct the equations for the expected return and standard deviation for the "total portfolio" which includes the portfolio of risky assets and the risk-free asset. (Portfolios which we discussed earlier which do not contain the risk-free asset will be called "risky portfolios" to distinguish them from total portfolios.)

Let　R_T　=　return on a total portfolio,

　　　R_R　=　return on a risky portfolio,

　　　R_{RF}　=　return on the risk free asset,

and p = proportion of the total portfolio in the risk-free asset.

Then the expected return of the combined investment is given by

$$E(R_T) = p\, R_{RF} + (1 - p)\, E(R_R).$$

This is simply the weighted average of the risk free return and the expected return of the risky portfolio. The standard deviation of the total portfolio is given by

$$\sigma_T = (1-p)\, \sigma_R$$

where σ_R is the standard deviation of the risky portfolio. Since the standard deviation of the risk-free asset is zero, it does not appear in the equation and the correlation between it and any risky asset is also zero.

The addition of the risk free asset allows us to construct a new efficient set. This new efficient set can be shown in the following figure.

The line DF represents this new efficient set. The point D is plotted at the risk-free rate of return. The line DF is the line that passes thru D and is tangent to the efficient frontier at the point E and is the steepest possible line. The points on this line represent the total portfolios which are a combination of the risk-free asset and the portfolio of risky assets located at point E. Point D represents the portfolio where all funds are invested in

Figure 2.6   New Efficient Set with the Addition
of a Risk-Free Asset

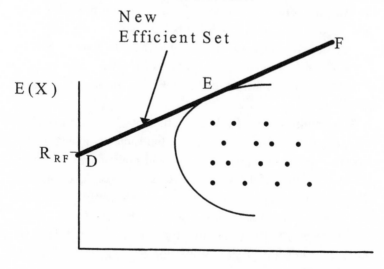

the risk-free asset. This would be equivalent to letting p equal 1.0. Point E represents the point where all the funds are invested in the risky portfolio. This is equivalent to letting p equal 0. The points in-between represent portfolios with a p between 0 and 1.

Points on the line segment EF are portfolios where the investor has borrowed funds at the risk-free rate and then used the additional funds to purchase more of the risky portfolio at E. This allows investors to obtain higher expected returns while assuming a higher risk. The values of p along this segment would be negative, reflecting the fact that the investor is borrowing at the risk-free rate.

Why does the line DF represent the new efficient set? Any investment approach for the total portfolio consisting of the risk-free asset and any feasible risky portfolio must lie along a line between the point D (risk-free asset) and that risky portfolio. Any line drawn from point D to any risky portfolio other than the one located at E, will be below the line DF. Therefore, line DF dominates any other attainable lines. In other words, for a given standard deviation the total portfolio with the highest expected value will fall on the line DF, thus forming the new efficient set.

The ramifications of this new efficient set are far-reaching. It implies that all investors that use the same estimates for the expected value, standard deviation, and covariances will have the same risky portfolio. The difference between investors will lie in what proportion of funds is in this risky portfolio and what is in the risk-free asset. This would be decided based on the risk-return preference of the investor. The less the risk level an investor desires, the greater proportion the risk free asset. This is equivalent to increasing p and places the investor closer to point D on the efficient set line DF.

This leads to what is known as the *separation property* or *separation theorem*. It states that the investment decision can be separated into two steps. The first step is to find the risky portfolio located at point E in the efficient set. This is the optimal risky portfolio everyone should hold. The next step is to determine the proportion of the total investment that is placed in the risky portfolio and what proportion is placed in the risk-free asset. This property essentially separates the problem of what risky securities make up the portfolio and how to allocate the funds between risky and non-risky assets.

THE SINGLE INDEX MODEL

One difficulty with using the Markowitz mean-variance method for portfolio selection is the complexity involved in computing the variances of the portfolios. Estimates for the covariances between all the securities being considered must be computed. The number of these covariances can become overwhelming. If n is the number of securities, then the general formula for the number of unique covariances is given by $[n(n - 1)]/2$. For example, if sixty securities are being considered then, $[60(60-1)]/2 = 1,770$ unique covariances must be estimated. Since a professional analyst might wish to consider hundreds of stocks, it becomes impractical to try to estimate all the necessary covariances. The following model will be one method which can be used to reduce the number quantities that need to be estimated.

The *single index model* was developed by William Sharpe.[2] It relates returns on a security to the percent change of a common index. The common index is usually a market index such as the Dow Jones Average or the S&P 500, but may be any index which is strongly correlated with securities. The model is given by the following equation:

$$R_i = \alpha_i + \beta_i I + e_i$$

In this model R_i represents the return on security i and I represents the percentage change of the index. The parameter α_i equals the portion of security i's return that is not related to the index and β_i equals the amount that security i's return, R_i, is expected to change given a one unit increase in the index, I. The quantity e_i is called the random error or residual, it equals the difference between the predicted return, R_i^*, as given by $R_i^* = \alpha_i + \beta_i I$ and the actual return R_i. The following numerical example will help illustrate how this model works.

Suppose a security has an α_i equal to 4% and β_i equal to 1.8. Also, the percent change for the index during the period of interest is 15%. Then the single index model would estimate the security's return to be $R_i^* = 4\% + 1.8(15\%) = 31\%$. Since this is only a prediction, the actual return is likely to be different, hopefully by only a small amount. Suppose the actual return, R_i, is equal to 34%. Then the residual error, or e_i, equals $R_i - R_i^* = 34\% - 31\% = 3\%$.

[2] William Sharpe, "A simplified Model for Portfolio Analysis," *Management Science*, January 1963, vol. 9, p 277–293.

The formulas to calculate α_i and β_i are given by

$$\beta_i = \frac{\text{covariance } (R_i I)}{\text{variance}(I)}$$

and $\qquad \alpha_i = \overline{R}_i - \beta_i \overline{I}.$

Where $\overline{R}_i$ is the average return on security i and $\overline{I}$ is the average percent change in the index. These quantities are usually estimated by historical data using a statistical technique called regression analysis.

The parameter β_i is very important. When the index used in the model is a market index, such as the S&P 500, β_i is known as the "beta" in the popular literature. Since it quantifies how much the return of a security fluctuates in relation to movements in the market, it is used as a measure of systematic risk. This will be discussed in detail in the next chapter, the important concept for now is to understand how the single index model can be used to simplify the calculations for the variance of a portfolio.

In order to use the single index model to simplify the calculations a critical assumption must be made. It is assumed that the securities are related to each other only through the common index I. In other words, any relationship in their movements is because of their common relationship with the index. Statistically, this is equivalent to stating that the residual errors for any two securities i and j are independent or covariance $(e_i, e_j) = 0$. This assumption implies that if an event occurs that affects security i, but is not related to the common index, then the event has no affect on security j.

Finally, we can now write the covariance of security i and j as:

$$\sigma_{ij} = \beta_i \beta_j \sigma_I^2$$

This implies that to compute the covariance between any two securities all that is needed are the β's for each and the variance of the common index. This greatly reduces the number of quantities that need to be estimated for the Markowitz model. Earlier we saw that if an analyst wanted to consider just sixty securities, then the number of unique covariances that had to be estimated was 1,770. Using the single index model we need only to estimate the sixty β values and the variance of the common index, a much less onerous chore. This difference becomes even more dramatic as the number of securities being considered grows.

Another result from the single index model is the following alternative calculation for the variance σ_i^2 of a security.

$$\sigma_i^2 = \beta_i^2(\sigma_I^2) + \sigma_{e_i}^2$$

This basically partitions the total risk of a security, as measured by its variance into two components. The first component, $\beta_i^2(\sigma_I^2)$, reflects the common index or market risk of the security. This is the portion of the variance due to movements in the index. The other component, $\sigma_{e_i}^2$, reflects the security specific risk. This portion measures the variability which is unique to that security.

SYSTEMATIC AND NONSYSTEMATIC RISKS

Since the goal of portfolio selection is to obtain a desired expected return at the lowest possible risk, the question arises as to how low can the risk or standard deviation of a portfolio be made. This brings us to the concepts of systematic and nonsystematic risk. Using the results from the single index model, we can write the variance of a portfolio as

$$\sigma_p^2 = \beta_p^2(\sigma_I^2) + \sigma_{e_p}^2$$

The quantity $\beta_p^2(\sigma_I^2)$ is the market risk or what is called the *systematic risk*. The term $\sigma_{e_p}^2$ is called the *nonsystematic risk* of the portfolio. The systematic risk is the amount of variance in the portfolio that is related to general movements in the market. Since this risk reflects how the securities within the portfolio covary together it cannot be diversified away. On the other hand, the nonsystematic risk reflects the variance which is not correlated to the market and is a function of the unique risks of the individual securities. Therefore, this nonsystematic risk can be diversified away. Some securities will randomly increase while others will decrease and so these nonsystematic fluctuations will tend to cancel each other out.

The following graph shows what generally happens to the total risk of a portfolio as the number of securities increases.

As we can see in the graph, the nonsystematic risk decreases as the number of securities in the portfolio increases. So the total risk decreases, but not below the systematic risk. The nonsystematic risk can be diversified away, but no matter how many securities are included, the systematic risk remains.

This result has important implications when considering what risk an investor should be concerned with when pricing a security. In a portfolio, which contains many securities, the relevant measure of risk for an individual security in the portfolio should only reflect the systematic risk, since the nonsystematic risk can be diversified away. As we will see in the next chapter,

Figure 2.7   Portfolio Risk versus Number of Securities

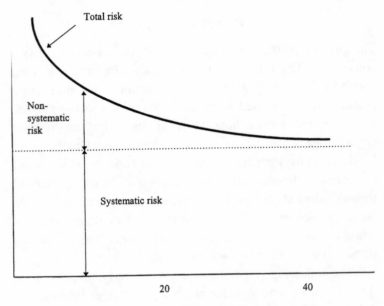

Number of Securities in the Portfolio

this helps to explain why "beta" becomes such an important measure of risk.

End Note

[i] If the random variables X_i and X_j take on are discrete (i.e. the values can be listed), this formula is equivalent to:

$$\sigma_{ij} = \sum_{all\,x\,i}\sum_{all\,x\,j} (x_i - \mu_i)(x_j - \mu_j)\,P(x_i,x_j)$$

where, $P(x_i, x_j)$ = joint probability of X_i and X_j.

Note that x_i and x_j represent particular returns for securities X_i and X_j.

3

BETA AND
CAPITAL MARKETS

BETA

While investigating the stocks for Microsoft, Gillette, and AT&T on the Internet in May of 1998, an investor comes across a quantity called beta. It is listed along with the price, P/E ratio, dividend, and other measures which aid the investor in making decisions concerning the stock. The beta for Microsoft was 1.27, for Gillette it was 1.02, and for AT&T it was 0.66. What do these numbers mean and what information are they giving us?

The concept of beta was developed to help investors compare the risk of a risky asset to the market as a whole. The risky asset could be a stock, a portfolio, or a mutual fund. As a proxy for the market, an index such as the Standard and Poor 500 is usually used. Beta provides the investor with a measure of how volatile the asset is relative to the market index.

Beta is estimated by fitting a statistical linear regression equation. A linear regression models the relationship between two variables as a straight line. The two variables are usually referred to as the dependent and independent variable. In a graph, the dependent variable is plotted along the vertical axis and the independent variable is plotted along the horizontal axis. Recall from algebra that a straight line is determined by two parameters, an intercept and a slope. The intercept is usually denoted by the Greek letter alpha, α. It is the point where the regression line cuts the vertical axis, or the value of the dependent variable when the independent variable equals zero. The slope is usually denoted by the Greek letter beta, β. It measures the steepness of the line. An important interpretation of the slope is that it measures the number of units that the dependent variable changes for each unit that the independent variable changes.

The beta that investors are concerned with is based on estimating the following linear regression equation, called the *characteristic line*.

$$\hat{R} = \hat{\alpha} + \hat{\beta}R_M$$

The "^" over a quantity means that it is an estimate of that quantity. Thus, $\hat{\alpha}$ and $\hat{\beta}$ are estimates of alpha and beta. To compute these estimates, observations must be taken over many periods of time. These periods could be any time interval for which returns are available—for example days, weeks, or months. The dependent variable R is the rate of return for a particular security. The quantity $\hat{R}$ is the fitted return of the particular security based on the model. The independent variable R_M is the return on the market index (referred to as I in the last chapter). The term $\hat{\alpha}$ is the estimated intercept and $\hat{\beta}$ is the estimated slope. Since this model, or any model, cannot be expected to perfectly duplicate the actual observed return of a security, an error term, e, is introduced to represent the difference between the fitted value, $\hat{R}$, and the actual observed value, R. Thus we have the model

$$R = \hat{R} + e$$

or $\qquad R = \hat{\alpha} = \hat{\beta}R_M + e.$

This model is displayed in the figure below.

The statistical procedure used to estimate the parameters α and β minimizes the sum of the squares of each of the vertical distances between the actual point and the regression line. This

Figure 3.1   Fitting the Characteristic Line

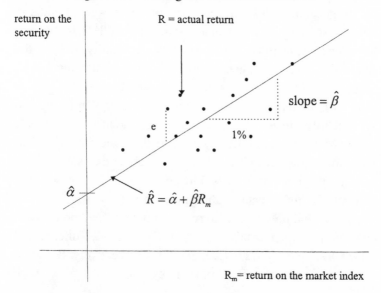

procedure is called the least squares fit. Standard statistical soft-
ware packages or spreadsheet packages can be used to calculate
the estimates.

How do we interpret the value of beta? Since it is the slope
of the model, it represents the estimated change in the return of
the security for one unit change in the return of the market index. For example, suppose the beta for a stock is 2.0. This implies that for each increase (or decrease) of 1 in the rate of
return of the market index there is an estimated increase (or decrease) of 2 in the rate of return in the security. In this case we
would say that the security is riskier than the market index since
its volatility is twice as great. Alternatively, if the beta is 0.5,
then the security has less risk than the market index. In this
case, if the market index's return increases (or decreases) by 1
then the security's estimated return would increase (or decrease)
by only 0.5.

In general, if the beta for a security is between 0 and 1.0,
then the security is said to be less risky or volatile than the market. This is sometimes called a defensive security, since it de-
fends the investor against high volatility in the market. A
security with a beta greater than 1.0 is said to be more risky or
more volatile than the market. This would be called an aggressive security, since it fluctuates more than the market. Finally, a
security with a beta of 1.0 would have the same risk or volatility as the market since it would fluctuate about the same amount
as does the market. This would be called a neutral security.
Overall, the higher beta implies a greater risk.

We should now be able to return to our original three stocks
and interpret their beta's. Recall that Microsoft, Gillette, and
AT&T had betas of 1.27, 1.02, and 0.66, respectively. Based on
these values, Microsoft is most risky, since it is 27% more

volatile than the market. Gillette is the closest to the market, with a beta that's nearly one. Finally, AT&T is less volatile than the market, its beta is less than one.

The theoretical foundation for beta, as the measure of relevant risk when pricing a security, lies in the Capital Asset Pricing Model.

CAPITAL ASSET PRICING MODEL

In the 1960s, William Sharpe—who won the 1990 Nobel Prize in Economics—John Lintner, and Jan Mossin developed the Capital Asset Pricing Model (CAPM).[1] The model attempts to quantify the relationship between the risk and the expected return of risky assets. In so doing it establishes the price of the asset when the market is in equilibrium. Market equilibrium implies that the prices have settled at a level where there is no apparent gain to buy or sell one asset for another, after taking into account risk. In order to develop the CAPM, other assumptions besides market equilibrium are made: all investors use the Markowitz portfolio model, discussed earlier, to determine their portfolio selection and all have the same inputs i.e. the expectations, variances and covariances of the returns. Other assumptions for all investors include no transactions costs and the availability of funds to borrow or lend at the risk-free rate.

Under these assumptions all investors will hold the same

[1] Sharpe, W. (1964), "Capital Asset Prices: A Theory of Market Equilibrium under Conditions of Risk," *Journal of Finance*, 88, 425–442.

Litner, John (1965), "The Valuation of Risk Assets and the Selection of Risky Investments in Stock Portfolio and Capital Budgets," *Review of Economics and Statistics* pp.13–36.

Mossin, Jan (1966), "Equilibrium in a Capital Asset Market," *Econometric*.

optimal risky portfolio. What is the reasoning behind this? Since all investors use the same inputs and criteria to find the optimal risky portfolio, they will all decide on the same risky portfolio. The only variable they differ on will be their risk preferences. Recall from the separation theorem of the last chapter that the risk preference of the individual investor does not influence the selection of the optimal risky portfolio. It is taken into account when the decision is made as to the allocation of funds between the risk-free asset and the optimal risky portfolio. What is this ultimate risky portfolio? It is the portfolio which contains all available risky assets. This includes all stocks, bonds, international securities, etc. Clearly, this ultimate portfolio, which is called the *market portfolio*, does not exist in reality, but only in theory. Usually a broad-based index such as the S&P 500 index is used as a proxy for it.

A major result of the CAPM is the *security market line(SML)*. The SML displays the relationship between expected return and risk for any security or portfolio and is given by the following equation:

$$E\,(R) = R_{RF} + \beta\,[E(R_M) - R_{RF}].$$

In this equation $E(R)$ is the expected return of the asset, R_{RF} is the risk free rate of return, and β (beta) is our measure of risk. Thus the term $\beta\,[E(R_M) - R_{RF}]$ is the risk premium for the asset. Notice that $E(R_M)$ and R_{RF} are the same for all assets, so the greater the beta the greater the expected value. Therefore, if CAPM is correct, beta is the relevant measure of risk when determining the expected value of the asset.

For a computational example, let's use the SML to find the expected return for Microsoft. Recall that its beta was 1.27. Now suppose that the risk free-rate of return is 5% and the expected return on the market is 12%. Based on the SML, the expected return of Microsoft should be equal to

$$E(R) = 5\% + 1.27[12\% - 5\%] = 13.89\%.$$

It is higher than the market return since it is considered riskier than the market portfolio. This expected return is also called the *required rate of return*, it is the return an investor "requires" for that level of risk.

The SML can be used to help the investor determine the equilibrium price of a security, hence the word "pricing" in the name Capital Asset Pricing Model. Suppose that based on a method other than CAPM, the expected return on an asset is higher than what the SML provides. The CAPM is now telling us that this security is undervalued. Why? If the expected return is higher than it should be based on the risk level, then more investors will seek out this asset and buy more of it. This will drive the price higher until it reaches the equilibrium point based on the CAPM. At this point the new expected return will have dropped, since the current price will have increased and the end of the period price will have remained the same. Conversely, if the expected return is determined to be lower than what is given by the SML, then the CAPM indicates that this asset is overvalued. In this case, investors will sell the asset since they are not being compensated enough for the high risk. This will cause the price to drop until the expected return settles at the equilibrium point on the SML. The following graph of the SML illustrates an undervalued and overvalued asset.

The SML slopes upward, as expected, since a greater beta demands a greater expected return. When beta equals 0, which implies no systematic risk, the expected return is equal to the risk free return, R_{RF}. If an asset has a beta of 1, then the expected

Figure 3.2   The Security Market Line

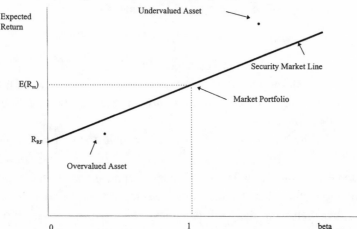

return equals the expected market return. For a beta less than 1, the asset's expected return is less than the market portfolio's expected return. Conversely, if its beta is greater than 1, then its expected return is greater than the market portfolio.

It is important to remember that the CAPM is a mathematical model that tries to approximate the market. It is based on assumptions that may be unrealistic, but the real question is how close it comes to reality. Many empirical studies have been performed, and the results are inconclusive. In fact, it has been argued that that model can never be proven.[2] Although it has these weaknesses, the CAPM does provide the investor with insights into how risk should be measured and the relationship it has to the expected return.

[2] See Richard Roll (1977), "A Critique of the Asset Pricing Theory's Tests: Part I: On Past and Potential Testability of the Theory," *Journal of Financial Economics*, Vol. 4, pp. 129–176.

THE ARBITRAGE PRICING THEORY

Other models besides the CAPM have been proposed to model the pricing of securities. The Arbitrage Pricing Theory (APT), which was developed by Stephen Ross,[3] is one such alternative in the pricing of securities. This section presents a brief description of the model, with the intent to make the reader aware of this theory and to give a few of the basic concepts. Several excellent references, which give a more detailed and complete description of the theory, are listed in the selected bibliography.

The APT, like the CAPM, develops a model that describes the relationship between the expected return and the risk of a security. One of the main differences between the models lies in their assumptions. The APT has less restrictive assumptions than does CAPM. For example, it does not assume that all investors use Markowitz's mean-variance criteria for portfolio selection.

The APT uses several indexes or factors rather than just one. The CAPM uses only the market portfolio, where the APT can use several factors or indexes, whichever are necessary to help explain the systematic risk of the securities. The APT hypothesizes that the expected returns are not sensitive to just one type of systematic risk, but to several different types of risks.

The problem with APT is that it does not tell us which risks

---

[3] Stephen A. Ross (1976), "The Arbitrage Theory of Capital Asset Pricing," *Journal of Economic Theory*, 13, no. 3, pp. 341–360.

should be used. Berry, Burmeister, and McElroy suggest the following five factors:[4]

- risk of changes in default premiums,
- risk that the term structure of interest rates may change,
- risk of unanticipated inflation or deflation,
- risk that the long-run expected growth rate of profits for the economy will change, and
- residual market risk, or any remaining risk needed to explain a market index such as the S&P 500.

These risk factors measure the surprise or unanticipated changes between the actual value and expected value. For example, inflation is not a risk factor, but unanticipated inflation is one. Berry et al. state that variables which are legitimate risk factors must have the following three properties:

1. At the beginning of every period, the factor must be completely unpredictable to the market.
2. Each APT factor must have a pervasive influence on stock returns.
3. Relevant factors must influence expected return; i.e., they must have non-zero prices.

Thus, the risk factors cannot be predicted, they cannot be specific to an individual security, and they must contain useful information affecting expected return.

[4] Michael A. Berry, Edwin Burmeister, and Marjorie B. McElroy, "Sorting Out Risks Using Known APT Factors," *Financial Analysis Journal*, March-April 1988, pp. 29–42.

The APT is an equilibrium model, since it estimates what prices should be assuming no arbitrage opportunities. An arbitrage opportunity occurs if an investor can make a risk-free gain from that opportunity. The following is a simple example of an arbitrage opportunity. Suppose an investor could borrow money at one bank at 5% and then deposit the money into another bank which pays 6% interest. In this case the investor would make 1% on all moneys borrowed, risk-free. This situation could not possibly exist for long, since many investors would take advantage of it. With many investors borrowing large sums from the first bank, it would either raise the rate until the rate settled at an equilibrium level or run out of funds to lend.

Finally, the following is an equation which results from the APT.

$$R = E(R) + \beta_1 F_1 + \beta_2 F_2 + ... + \beta_n F_n + e,$$

where R = the return for the security of interest,

$E(R)$ = the expected return of the security,

F_i = the ith risk factor (i.e. the unanticipated change in inflation),

and β_i = the sensitivity of the security to factor F_i.

Multiple Regression, which is an extension of simple linear regression, can be used to fit this type of model.

4

MEASURING
PERFORMANCE

On Monday, October 27, 1997, the Dow (Dow Jones Industrial Average) fell 554 points, the greatest point drop in history. But what is the meaning of such a drop? Approximately ten years earlier, on "Black Monday," October 18, 1987, the Dow fell by 508 points, almost the same amount. Do these two drops have the same meaning to an investor? One way to compare the Dow's performance for these two days is to compute the percent change in value for each day. For October 27, 1997, the greatest point drop in history, the drop was seven percent. For "Black Monday," the drop was twenty-three percent, over three times greater! Clearly, it is important for an investor to consider the percent change as well as the point drop.

In this chapter, we will examine how to measure the performance of investments. The rate of return is the most quoted and most easily understood performance measure. Whether it be a particular stock, a portfolio of stocks, bonds, or other securities, it is a basic quantity that concerns every investor. We will first consider the simplest case of a single period rate of return. This was the situation in the previous large drops in the Dow. The case of a portfolio with several assets is then considered, where the rate of return will become a weighted average.

Next we look at the more complicated case of multiple periods. Here we will see that there are several ways to compute the rate of return: the arithmetic mean and the geometric mean. We will see how to compute both, and discuss the differences.

A drawback to the rate of return as a measure of performance is that it does not take into account the risk of the investment. So to use it as the sole criteria could be misleading. For example, suppose we wish to compare the performance of two equity funds. One fund may have taken enormous risks and predicted (or guessed) correctly. Thus, it had a very high rate of return. The second fund was more conservative, took less risks and had a lower rate of return. In this case, the rate of return by itself does not tell the full story. It does not reflect the different risk levels and investment strategies of the two funds. The investor would be prudent to take into account other factors besides the rate of return, such as the risk and investment objectives, when evaluating performance. The last section will provide several performance measures which will adjust for the risk.

RATE OF RETURN FOR ONE PERIOD

Suppose you are comparing two investments. The first was an investment of $1,000 which grew to $1,100, the other was a $10,000 investment which grew to $10,100. Both investments grew by $100, but intuitively, the first investment is preferable, since it has a much less initial investment. Therefore, it is important to quantify the return in terms of a percentage growth, i.e. rate of return, rather than in absolute dollars. The rate of return for the $1,000 investment was 10%, whereas the rate of return for the $10,000 investment was only 1%.

The rate of return over one period of time can be defined by the equation:

$$\text{rate of return} = \frac{\text{ending value} - \text{initial investment}}{\text{initial investment}}$$

The initial investment is the value of the investment at the beginning of the period, usually the purchase price. The ending value is the total value of the investment at the end of the period. Thus, the numerator is simply the change in value of the investment. This change in value may occur because of an appreciation (or depreciation) of the assets, which would be reflected in an increase (or decrease) in the price at the end of the period. Also, income such as interest or dividends will affect the ending value.

Let's compute the rates of return for our two previous examples. Recall that the first investment had an initial value of $1,000 and an ending value of $1,100. Therefore, the rate of return equals (1,100 − 1,000)/1,000 = .10 or 10%. Similarly, the rate of return for the second investment would be (10,100 − 10,000)/10,000 = .01 or 1%.

For another example, consider purchasing stock in the Chrysler Corporation. Suppose you purchased 200 shares on January 2, 1997 at a price of $33 per share and then sold all 200 shares one year later on January 2, 1998 at a price of 35 3/16 per share. During the year you received $320 in dividends. What would be your rate of return for this investment? For now we will not worry about the commissions for buying and selling the stock.

Initial Investment	= (# of shares) X (price per share)
	= (200) X (33)
	= $6,600
Ending Value	= (# of shares) X (price per share) + dividends
	= (200) X (35 3/16) + 320
	= $7,357.50
Rate of Return	= (7,357.50 − 6,600) / 6,600
	= .115 or 11.5%

There are several adjustments we should consider making to the above calculations. First we may want to take into account the commissions to buy and sell the stock. We would not make this adjustment if we already owned the stock and did not actually sell it. But if we did, then the true return on our investment would be lower than the one calculated above. Suppose we paid a commission of $35 when we purchased the stock and $30 when we sold the stock.[1] The following shows how to incorporate these commissions into the calculation for the rate of return.

Initial Investment	= (# of shares) X (price per share) + commission
	= (200) X (33) + 35
	= $6,635
Ending Value	= (# of shares) X (price per share) + dividends − commission

[1] Usually the commission to buy and sell the stock is the same, here we made them unequal to clearly illustrate how they are used in the computations.

$$= (200) \text{ X } (35^3/_{16}) + 320 - 30$$
$$= \$7,327.50$$

Rate of Return $\quad = (7,327.50 - 6,635) / 6,635$
$$= .104 \text{ or } 10.4\%$$

Accounting for the commissions, the rate of return is 10.4%, which is somewhat lower than the 11.5%. The impact of the commission is dependent upon the size of the commission relative to the size of the investment. This is important to keep in mind, especially in today's stock market, since many discount brokers charge the same fee no matter how many shares are bought or how large is the dollar amount of the investment.[2] For example, suppose we had purchased the Chrysler stock as described in the previous example, but we purchased 400 shares instead of 200. Assuming the commissions stay the same, the rate of return would be 11.0% instead of 10.4%, a slightly better return.

The above computations do not take into account the time value of the dividends. They are correct as long as the dividends occur at the end of the period or if they are not reinvested during the period. Later, we will see how to account for the time value of the dividends.

WEIGHTED AVERAGE RATE OF RETURN

An investor may have several investments, each with its own rate of return, and wish to compute an overall rate of return. This may be done by computing a weighted average of the

---

[2] Some limits are usually placed on orders, based on this flat fee, but these limits are so high that they usually do not affect most individual investors.

rates where the weights are based on the initial investment. For example, suppose a total initial investment of $35,000 is distributed into three investments as given below.

Investment	Initial Investment	Rate of Return
A	$10,000	12%
B	$ 5,000	8%
C	$20,000	20%

The overall rate of return can be computed in the following manner:

rate of return = [(10,000)(.12) + (5,000)(.08) + (20,000)(.20)]/35,000 = .16 or 16%.

RATE OF RETURN FOR MULTIPLE PERIODS

Arithmetic Mean

What happens when the investment spans several periods? Suppose we have yearly returns for an investment over several years and we wish to compute a rate of return per year that best represents the performance of that investment. There are two methods that can be used: the first, the arithmetic mean, is the simplest and easiest understood measure. The *arithmetic mean or average*, $\bar{R}$, is the sum of the yearly rates of return divided by the number of years. The formula is given by

$$\bar{R} = \frac{R_1 + R_2 + \dots + R_n}{n}.$$

Where R_i equals the return for the ith year and n equals the number of years. For example, suppose a fund had the following rates of return.

Year	Rate of Return
1	25%
2	15%
3	-10%
4	20%

Then the arithmetic mean equals:

$$\bar{R} = \frac{25\% + 15\% - 10\% + 20\%}{4} = 12.5\%$$

Thus, 12.5% may be thought of as a typical return for one year.

Geometric Mean

The *geometric mean* is an alternative to the arithmetic mean in computing the rate of return over multiple periods. It is the constant rate of growth per year which would yield the equivalent return as the series of actual observed rates. The following equation illustrates this equivalence:

$$(1 + R_G)(1 + R_G) \dots (1 + R_G) = (1 + R_1)(1 + R_2) \dots (1 + R_n)$$
$$(n \; times)$$

or,

$$(1 + R_G)^n = (1 + R_1)(1 + R_2) \dots (1 + R_n)$$

where R_G is the geometric mean and, as before, R_i is the rate of return for the ith year (but in decimal form) and n is the number of years. Notice that 1 has been added to all the rates before they are multiplied together. The reason for this is that if R is the rate of return for a period then $(1 + R)$ is the factor that is multiplied to the amount at the beginning of the period in order to get the amount at the end of the period.

Taking the above equation and solving for R_G, we get;

$$R_G = [(1 + R_1) (1 + R_2) \ldots (1 + R_n)]^{1/n} - 1.$$

To illustrate how to use this equation, we will compute the geometric mean for the same fund example that we used to illustrate the arithmetic mean.

$$
\begin{aligned}
R_G &= (1 + .25)(1 + .15)(1 - .10)(1 + .20)^{1/4} - 1 \\
&= .116 \\
&\quad or \\
&= 11.6\%
\end{aligned}
$$

Arithmetic versus Geometric Mean

Notice that in our previous example the geometric mean, $R_G = 11.6\%$, is less than the arithmetic average, $\overline{R} = 12.5\%$. Why? The geometric mean measures the compound rate of change of the investment. In other words, the geometric mean equals the constant rate change needed for an investment to grow over multiple periods to equal the actual realized ending value. The arithmetic mean does not take into account this compounding and simply attempts to find the typical rate of change over a single period. The following extreme but simple example illustrates this point. Suppose we invested $200 for two years. During the first year, the investment halved in value or decreased by 50% and the second year it doubled or grew by 100%. These rates of return and the value of the $200 investment at the end of each year is given in the following table, along with the computations for the arithmetic and geometric mean.

Year	Annual Rate of Return	Value At Year End
1	−50%	$200(1−50%)=$100
2	+100%	$100(1+100%)=$200

arithmetic mean $\bar{R} = \dfrac{(-50\%) + (100\%)}{2} = 25\%$

geometric mean $= R_G = [(1 - .50)(1 + 1.00)]^{1/2} - 1 = 0\%.$

The arithmetic mean of 25% does not seem to be a reasonable measure of performance since the investment initially had a value of $200 and an ending value of $200. Having a mean of 25% implies that the investment grew, which it did not. The geometric mean of 0% seems to be more appropriate. It takes into account the fact that when it doubled in value, this increase is only on its halved value. Thus, they balance out for an overall return of 0%.

When would the arithmetic mean be more appropriate to use? Suppose we wanted to forecast the rate of return for the next period based on previous returns. In this case, the arithmetic mean would be more appropriate, since it measures the return of a typical single period. Even in the previous case, if we wished to predict the return for the next year, it can be reasoned that 25% is the better prediction than 0%.

If the rates of return each period are the same, then the arithmetic and geometric means will be equal and it will not matter which is used. As the returns per period become more varied, the difference between the two measures will become more prominent.

INTERNAL RATE OF RETURN

Up to this point we have only considered the case where there has been an initial investment and no moneys have been added or withdrawn from it during the entire time of interest. If money is added or withdrawn at different times, it becomes much more difficult to compute a measure of performance or rate of return since the time value of money should be taken into consideration. The *internal rate of return (IRR)* is used in this case, where money is flowing in and out of the investment. It uses a discounted cash flow method to obtain an annual rate of return. Each cash flow is discounted to obtain its present value. The equation needed to obtain the present value of an amount is obtained from the compound amount formula:

$$\text{amount} = (\text{present value})(1+\text{rate})^n$$

This computes the amount a sum of money (i.e. present value) will grow to at a constant rate per period for *n* periods. It assumes the money is compounded from period to period. Taking this equation and solving for the present value we get:

$$\text{present value} = \frac{\text{amount}}{(1+\text{rate})^n}$$

This is the formula that we will use to find the present value of each of the cash flows.

The internal rate of return is based on finding the rate to satisfy the condition that the sum of the present value of the outflows (or payments) is equal to the sum of the present value of the inflows (or income). This is equivalent to adding the present value of the cash flows, where the cash flow equals income minus payment, and then setting the sum to zero. The following is the equation used to find the internal rate of return.

$$0 = \text{CF}_0 + \frac{\text{CF}_1}{(1 + \text{IRR})^1} + \frac{\text{CF}_2}{(1 + \text{IRR})^2} + \cdots + \frac{\text{CF}_n}{(1 + \text{IRR})^n}$$

The terms CF_0, CF_1, . . . CF_n are the cash flows (income – payment) at the end of periods 0, 1, . . ., n.

The following example illustrates how to set up the equation to solve for the internal rate of return. Suppose we first purchase ten shares of a stock for $100 per share. One year later, these shares of stock pay a total of $25 in dividends. The next year the total dividend is $40 and we purchase an additional five shares at $120 per share. Finally, at the end of the third year from our initial purchase, the stock pays us a total dividend of $60 and we sell all fifteen shares of the stock for $140 per share. What would our internal rate of return equal? Note that if we did not actually sell the stock in the end, for purposes of computing the cash flow we would act as if we did since the ending value of the investment should be thought of as income. These events are summarized in the following table, along with the computations for the cash flows.

End of Year	Event	CF= Cash Flow
0	Initial Payment = 10($100)=$1,000	– 1,000
1	Dividend Income = $25	+25
2	Dividend Income = $40	40 – 600 = -560
	Payment = 5($120) = $600	
3	Dividend Income = $60	60 + 2,100 = 2,160
	Income = 15($140)= $2,100	

Thus, IRR must satisfy the equation:

$$0 = -1,000 + \frac{25}{(1 + IRR)^1} + \frac{-560}{(1 + IRR)^2} + \frac{2,160}{(1 + IRR)^3}$$

Unfortunately, there is no closed form algebraic formula for IRR. Therefore, some numerical technique must be used to approximate IRR. Some financial calculators and computer spreadsheets have built in functions to compute the IRR. They usually use a mathematical iterative technique such as Newton's Method. If none of these are available, we could program a spreadsheet with the equation and then by trial and error approximate the IRR.

For our example we will use a Microsoft Excel spreadsheet, which has a built-in function to compute the IRR. The syntax of the function is

IRR(values, guess)

where, "values" is an array or reference of cells that contain the cash flows and "guess" is an initial estimate for IRR. You are not required to supply a guess. If omitted, it is taken to be .10.

For our example, the cash flows −1000, +25, −560, and 2160 were inputted into the cells A1, A2, A3, and A4, respectively. Then in another cell was typed "=IRR(A1:A4)," which returned a value of 16%. Therefore the internal rate of return for our investment is 16%. Our investment would have to grow by 16% each year to obtain the realized returns.

For more insight into understanding the internal rate of return, we note that in the simple case where there is only the initial payment and an ending value with no intervening cash flows, the internal rate of return and the geometric mean will be identical. See endnote for details.[i] Thus, much of our discussion concerning the geometric mean can be applied to the internal rate of return.

TIME WEIGHTED VERSUS DOLLAR WEIGHTED RETURNS

The internal rate of return is a *dollar weighted* approach to measuring performance. The return is dependent on the timing and size of the cash inflows and outflows. In some cases we do not want the measure of performance to have this property. For example, we may wish to compare mutual fund managers, who do not control when or how much individual investors will deposit or withdraw cash from their funds. An alternative to the dollar weighted approach is a *time-weighted* approach. This method computes the market value of the portfolio just before each cash flow. Then a rate of return is computed for each period between the cash flows. Finally, if the cash flows occur during the year, these rates of return can be linked in a compound or geometric fashion.

The following example demonstrates how to obtain a time-weighted rate of return. We will consider a stock investment where there are semi-annual cash flows, and we wish to obtain an annual rate of return. We will first compute the rate of return for each semi-annual period using both methods and then we will demonstrate how to convert these semi-annual rates to an annual rate.

Suppose that initially ten shares are purchased at $100 per share. After six months the stock drops in value, and the price per share is $90. At this time fifteen additional shares are purchased. At the end of the year, or after another six month period, the price per share rises to $150. These events are summarized below. Also shown are the cash flows and the market value of the investment just before and after each cash flow. The market values will be used to compute the time weighted rate of return and the cash flows will be used to compute the dollar weighted rate of return.

Beginning of first semi-annual period:
Cash Flow = − Payment = −(10 shares) ($100 per share)
$\qquad$ = −$1,000
Market Value = (10 shares)($100 per share) = $1,000

End of first semi-annual period:
Market Value = (10 shares) ($90 per share) = $900

Beginning of second semi-annual period:
Cash Flow = − Payment = −(15 shares)($90 per share)
$\qquad$ = −$1,350
Market Value = (25 shares) ($90 per share) = $2,250

End of second semi-annual period:
Cash Flow = Market Value = (25 shares) ($150 per share)
$\qquad$ = $3,750

Computations for time-weighted rate of return:

Rate for first semi-annual period $\quad$ = (900 − 1,000)/1,000
$\qquad\qquad\qquad\qquad\qquad\qquad$ = −10%

Rate for second semi-annual period = (3,750 − 2,250)/2,250
$\qquad\qquad\qquad\qquad\qquad\qquad$ = 67%

Computations for dollar-weighted rate of return (IRR):

$$0 = -1000 - 1{,}350/(1+IRR) + 3{,}750/(1+IRR)^2$$

Using Excel we find IRR = 38% (this is the rate per semi-annual period)

To convert these semi-annual rates into annualized rates, we assume compounding during the year. In general, for any number of interim periods during the year, we have the following equation

$$\text{annual rate} = [(1 + R_1)(1 + R_2)...(1 + R_n)] - 1$$

where R_1, R_2, and R_n are the interim rates per period and n is the number of periods per year. This equation is similar to the equation for the geometric mean. The reason is that both are based on compounding from period to period. The difference is that the geometric mean is finding the "mean" rate per period, whereas in this case we are "linking" the rates per interim period to obtain an overall annual rate. This is why the geometric mean raises the product $[(1 + R_1)(1 + R_2) \ldots (1 + R_n)]$ to the power 1/n, whereas the annual rate formula does not.

Using the previous annual rate formula we can now compute the annual rate of return based on time-weighted and dollar-weighted rates for our example.

annual rate based on time-weighted rates
$$= [(1 - .10)(1 + .67)] - 1$$
$$= 50\%$$

annual rate based on dollar-weighted rates
$$= [(1 + .38)(1 + .38)] - 1$$
$$= 90\%$$

In this example, notice the significant difference between the two rates. The dollar-weighted rate is much higher. Why? During the first semi-annual period, when there was a decrease in the value of the stock, the amount of dollars invested was less than during the second semi-annual period, when the stock surged. The dollar-weighted rate reflects this fact. The time-weighted method is not affected by the dollar amount, rather it only measures the rate of change between cash flows.

Which method should be used? This depends on the objective of the performance measure. If an investor is attempting to measure her own performance, then she should use the dollar-weighted method. She makes the decision when and how much to invest. So she should be rewarded if she invests more money when the investment's performance is good. On the other hand, if we wish to measure the performance of a fund manager who does not control the cash flows in and out of a fund, the time-weighted method is preferred. In this case, the fund manager should not be rewarded or penalized based on the dollar amount that the fund has during any particular period.

PERFORMANCE MEASURES ADJUSTED FOR RISK

In some cases, using the rate of return as the sole measure of performance does not give the complete picture. Suppose we wish to compare two mutual funds or portfolios whose risk levels are very different. We would expect the rate of return to be higher for the riskier portfolio. Recall that an investor expects a higher return for taking a greater risk. So when we compare the performance of mutual funds it is customary to compare funds with similar risk characteristics. We would compare the rate of return of a small cap fund to other small cap funds, a bond fund to other bond funds, etc. But even with this categorizing, risk characteristics can still differ within each group. Thus, it would be informative to calculate risk adjusted measures of performance. In this section we discuss three such measures. These measures are based on the concepts of the capital assets pricing model that was discussed earlier.

Sharpe's Measure

Our first measure was proposed by William Sharpe in the mid 1960s.[3] It is defined to be the ratio of excess return to total risk and is given by

$$\frac{\bar{R}_P - \bar{R}_{RF}}{\sigma_p}$$

where $\bar{R}_P$ equals the average rate of return for portfolio P during a period of time and $\bar{R}_{RF}$ equals the average risk free rate of return during the same period of time. Thus, the numerator is the difference or excess average rate of return. The denominator is the standard deviation of the returns over the same period of time and used as the measure of total risk of the portfolio. This measure can be interpreted to be the excess return per unit of total risk. Portfolios can be ranked by this performance measure, where the higher the measure the better the performance. The following example illustrates how to compute Sharpe's Measure for three hypothetical mutual funds A, B, and C. The average returns and standard deviations, computed from historical data over some period of time, is given in the following table.

[3] William Sharpe, "Mutual Fund Performance," *Journal of Business*, January 1966 , pp. 119–138.

Mutual Fund	Average Return	Standard Deviation
A	20%	18%
B	15%	14%
C	18%	13%
Risk Free	7%	

Then for Mutual Fund A we have Sharpe's Measure equal to (20% - 7%)/18% = .72. Similarly, for Funds B and C we have .57 and .85, respectively. Thus, the ranking would look like the following.

Rank	Mutual Fund	Sharpe's Measure
1	C	.85
2	A	.72
3	B	.57

Notice that Mutual Fund A, which had the largest average rate of return, comes in second behind Mutual Fund C. Although C had a lower rate of return, its risk level or standard deviation was less. This lower standard deviation was enough to give it a higher performance measure based on risk.

Treynor's Measure

The next risk adjusted measure of performance we consider was developed by Jack Treynor in 1965.[4] Treynor's Measure is similar to Sharpe's except it uses systematic risk instead of total risk. Instead of the standard deviation, he uses the beta coeffi-

[4] Jack Treynor, "How to Rate Management of Investment Funds," *Harvard Business Review* 43 (January - February 1965), pp. 63–75.

cient which we discussed earlier. Recall that since beta measures how sensitive a portfolio is to the market index, we use it as a measure of systematic risk.

$$\text{Treynor's Measure} = \frac{\overline{R}_P - \overline{R}_{RF}}{\beta_P}$$

Treynor's Measure is identical to Sharpe's, except σ_P is replaced by β_P. Thus, Treynor's Measure is a ratio of average excess return to systematic risk. It can be interpreted to be the average excess return per unit of systematic risk.

Suppose the betas for three mutual funds discussed earlier are 1.6, 0.6, and 1.5 for A, B, and C respectively. These values would have to be computed based on historical data over the same period of time as the returns. Then for mutual fund A, Treynor's Measure of performance equals $(20 - 7)/1.6 = 8.1$. The table below shows the results for funds B and C and the ranking of the three funds based on Treynor's Measure.

Rank	Mutual Fund	Treynor's Measure
1	B	13.3
2	A	8.1
3	C	7.3

In this case mutual fund B beats A and C. The major reason for this is that its beta was so much smaller than the other two. This compensated for the smaller rate of return. In other words, mutual fund B's rate of return is very good compared to the other two, once we take into account it's much smaller systematic risk.

Jensen's Measure

Our third and final risk adjusted measure of performance was developed in 1968 by Michael Jensen.[5] His measure can be written in the following form:

$$Jensen's\ Measure = \alpha_p$$
$$= \bar{R}_P - [\bar{R}_{RF} + \beta_P(\bar{R}_M - \bar{R}_{RF})]$$

Jensen's measure is α_p, or alpha, which is the difference between the portfolio's average return and an estimate of the expected return as given by the capital asset pricing model. Recall that based on the CAPM the expected return for a portfolio can be modeled by

$$E\ (R_p) = R_{RF} + \beta_P[E(R_m) - R_{RF}].$$

Historical data can be used to estimate this model. We replace the expected values on the right hand side of the equation with the corresponding average values computed over a particular time period. This gives us the following estimate for the expected return:

$$\hat{E}\ (R_p) = [\bar{R}_{RF} + \beta_P(\bar{R}_M - \bar{R}_{RF})].$$

The "^" (hat) over E means that it is an estimate of the expected return based on the model.

Jensen's Measure, α_p, now takes the difference between the actual average return over the period of interest, $\bar{R}_M$, and the estimate of the expected return based on the CAPM, $\hat{E}\ (R_p)$, giving us the following:

[5]Michael Jensen, "The Performance of Mutual Funds in the Period 1945–1964," *Journal of Finance*, May 1968, pp. 389–415.

$$\alpha_P = \overline{R}_P - \hat{E}(R_P)$$

or,

$$\alpha_P = \overline{R}_P - [\overline{R}_{RF} + \beta_P(\overline{R}_M - \overline{R}_{RF})].$$

Therefore, Jensen's measure can be interpreted to be an estimate of the difference between the portfolio's actual performance and its expected performance based on its level of systematic risk. It measures the performance of the managed portfolio, P, relative to an unmanaged portfolio of equal risk. If it is a statistically significant positive value, it implies that the managed portfolio outperformed the unmanaged portfolio. If significantly negative, it implies the managed portfolio underperformed. If it is not significantly different from zero, it implies that the performance was about the same as an unmanaged portfolio of equal risk.

Jensen's measure, alpha, can be computed by a regression analysis. We encountered regression earlier when we discussed beta. In fact, the same regression analysis can estimate both alpha and beta. The following is another way of writing Jensen's model for alpha.

$$(\overline{R}_P - \overline{R}_{RF}) = \alpha_P + \beta_P(\overline{R}_M - \overline{R}_{RF})$$

Further, we can write the following regression model.

$$(R_P - R_{RF}) = \alpha_P + \beta_P(R_M - R_{RF}) + e$$

The term $(R_P - R_{RF})$ equals the excess return of the managed portfolio for a single period, and $(R_M - R_{RF})$ equals the market excess return for the same period. The term e is the error or white noise in the regression model. Thus, α_P is the intercept or constant of the model and β_p, as we found before, is the slope of the model.

There are several benefits with this formulation. First, it allows us to estimate both alpha and beta simultaneously using regression analysis. But we do require historical data which gives the returns on a per period basis in order to perform the analysis, rather than the aggregated averages.

Another benefit is that part of the standard regression analysis output is a statistical test of alpha to determine if it is significantly different from zero. We need to determine statistical significance since this is only an estimate of the "true" alpha and so contains some sampling error. Thus, if the estimated alpha is only slightly different from zero and this difference is not statistically significant, then it can be attributed to random noise, rather than a real difference from zero.

The area of portfolio performance measurement is extensive and complicated. Choosing the correct performance measurement may not always be obvious. It will depend on the objective of the investor and his or her concerns. For example, in choosing which risk adjusted measure to use, an investor has to decide whether total risk or systematic risk matters more. This in turn will depend on how the portfolio fits into an overall investment strategy.

Data collection and manipulation is also a major concern. For example, data should be obtained over a long period in order to get a fair representation of performance. The starting and stopping dates for data gathering can be selected to show superior results. We have even seen that the method used to compute the rate of return can give very different results. As a response to these and other concerns, the Association for Investment Management and Research (AIMR) has published a set of performance presentation standards for measuring investment performance.[6]

The purpose of this chapter was to introduce some common performance measures, show how to compute them and give some intuitive understanding of them. The reader is encouraged to select one or more of the books in the bibliography for further reading.

Endnotes

[i] In this simple case the internal rate of return equation takes on the following form.

$$0 = CF_0 + \frac{CF_n}{(1+IRR)^n}$$

Notice that the only cash flows are the initial payment, CF_0, and the ending value CF_n. All cash flows in between are zero. For this special case we will be able to solve for IRR. But first we must make use of the following relationship between CF_n and CF_0.

$$CF_n = -CF_0(1+R_1)(1+R_2) \ldots (1+R_n),$$

where R_1, R_2, . . . R_n are the rates of return for the period 1, 2, . . ., n. Note that CF_n is income so it must be positive, but CF_0 is a payment and so is negative. Thus, we must multiply CF_0 by $(-)$ to obtain the correct sign for CF_n.

We now take the first equation and replace CF_n with the appropriate expression, then solve for IRR.

$$0 = CF_0 \frac{CF_n}{(1+IRR)^n}$$

[6] *Performance Presentation Standards*, Association for Investment Management and Research, Charlottesville, VA. 1993.

$$0 = CF_0 + \frac{-CF_0(1 + R_1)(1 + R_2) \ldots (1 + R_n)}{(1 + IRR)^n} \quad \{\text{replace } CF_n\}$$

$$0 = 1 - \frac{(1 + R_1)(1 + R_2) \ldots (1 + R_n)}{(1 + IRR)^n} \quad \{\text{divided by } CF_0\}$$

$$(1 + IRR)^n = (1 + R_1)(1 + R_2) \ldots (1 + R_n)$$

$$IRR = [(1 + R_1)(1 + R_2) \ldots (1 + R_n)]^{1/n} - 1.$$

This is the equation for the geometric mean, R_G, and so for this special case $IRR = R_G$.

5

MATH BEHIND SOME INVESTMENT PLANNING

DOLLAR COST AVERAGING

A popular strategy for investing in securities or mutual funds is dollar cost averaging. With this method you invest a fixed amount of money at equal intervals of time. For example, you may invest $500 on the first of every month. The advantage of this method is you will purchase more shares when the price is lower and less shares when the price is higher. Many workers who contribute to a retirement fund are basically using a dollar cost averaging approach to investment. They have a fixed amount of money deducted from their salary and/or, if they are lucky, contributed by their employer on a regular basis. If this money is then invested immediately, this would be a form of dollar cost averaging.

Let's now demonstrate this strategy with the following example. Suppose you invest $300, excluding commission (just to keep things simple), each period. The table below gives the price of the stock and the number of shares purchased each period.

Period	Investment	Price per Share	# of shares
1	$300	$50	6
2	$300	$30	10
3	$300	$25	12
4	$300	$50	6
5	$300	$60	5
Total	$1,500		39 shares

The average price per share over the five periods is (50+30+25+50+60)/5 = $43. But you paid an average per share of only 1500/39 = $38. The reason for this is that more shares were purchased when the price was low (i.e. in period 3 you purchased 12 shares at $25 each) and fewer shares when the price was high (i.e. in period 5 you purchased 5 shares at $60 each).

One possible drawback with this strategy is high commissions. You will incur higher total commissions by buying small quantities of securities frequently rather than making one large purchase. One way to avoid this expense is by purchasing shares of no-load funds.

MIRACLE OF COMPOUNDING

How early should someone start to invest for retirement? The effect of compounding makes a convincing argument that the earlier the better. Let's compare two scenarios. Suppose Mary at age 25 began to invest $2,000 a year into a mutual fund. She continued this for ten years or until she reached age 35. She allowed the money to grow until she retired at age 65. John on the other hand started later. He began investing $2,000 per year at age 35 and continued for the next 30 years until he reached age 65. Who will have more at retirement Mary, who invested a total of $20,000 or John, who invested a total of $60,000? Mary will be the clear winner with a significantly larger retirement nest-egg.

The key formula needed to do the calculations is sometimes called the *amount of an annuity* formula. If p dollars are invested at the end of each period for n periods and earns a rate of return of r per period, then the total amount S at the end of n periods is

$$S = p \left[\frac{(1 + r)^n - 1}{r} \right]$$

This assumes that the returns are left in the investment to compound each period. We can use this formula to compute the amount Mary has at age 35. Throughout these calculations we will assume no taxes and no commissions or fees. These are not unrealistic assumptions since most people can take advantage of a 401(k) or similar retirement plan, where taxes are deferred and fees are usually minimal. Also we'll assume a conservative annual return of 10%. By age 35 Mary will have accumulated:

$$\text{Mary's accumulation at age 35} = 2{,}000 \left[\frac{(1 + .10)^{10} - 1}{.10} \right]$$

$$= \$31{,}875.$$

Recall that at this time she stops contributing, but allows her investment to grow for the next thirty years. To compute the amount she has at age 65 we use the compound amount formula, which we've encountered before. We want to compute how much $31,875 will grow to in 30 years at a rate of return of 10% per year.

$$\text{Mary's accumulation at age } 65 = (\$31,875) \times (1 + 0.10)^{30}$$
$$= \$556,200$$

This is a sizable amount when you consider her total investment was only $20,000.

To compute John's accumulation at age 65 we only need to use the annuity amount formula with number of payments equal to thirty.

$$\text{John's accumulation at age } 65 = 2,000 \left[\frac{(1 + .10)^{30} - 1}{.10} \right]$$

$$= \$328,988.$$

A substantial amount, but much less than Mary's.

Suppose Mary received a slightly better return of 12% per year. Then Mary's accumulation would be $1,051,503! Almost double of what she received when the return was 10%. This illustrates how critical a 1% or 2% difference in the rate of return can be over a long term investment.

These cases show the power of compounding and the importance of investing early for retirement.

6

INDEXES

Anyone who follows newspaper, radio or television news will often hear the value of one or more indexes. Two of the more common types of indexes reported are stock indexes and consumer price indexes. A stock index is not the value of any one particular stock, but is based on a selection or subset of stocks. An index can measure stock performance for an overall market, an individual industry or almost any other category of stocks. It can be used as a quick indicator of market performance or as a gauge by which to measure the performance of a portfolio or an individual stock. Mutual fund performances are almost always compared to indexes. Funds have even been created whose holdings are based on the makeup of an index. Vanguard's S&P 500 fund is an example of this and is a very popular fund with investors who desire a return tied to the performance of the market. The fund managers need not do any research on stock selection. They simply purchase the stocks that make up the index. For this reason management fees are very small for this type of fund.

An index does not tell us everything about the performance of the market, sector, or economy. However, it does give us some quick and useful information on which we can base decisions. A huge variety of indexes exist. There is an index to track almost any area of the market that can be defined. Some of the more popular broadbased stock indexes are the Dow Jones Industrial Average, the S&P 500, the NSADAQ, the Russell 1000 and the Russell 2000.

The Consumer Price Index is not a stock index, but is important to investors. Inflation should be considered when reviewing returns from an investment, especially if the investment was made over a long period of time. The Consumer Price Index is one possible measure that is used to adjust for inflation.

DOW JONES INDUSTRIAL AVERAGE

The grandmother of all stock indexes is the Dow Jones Industrial Average (DJIA) devised by Charles Dow over one hundred years ago. In 1882, Charles Bergstresser helped finance Charles Dow and Edward Jones in a publishing venture and then became their partner. With the help of messenger boys, the firm gathered news and distributed it. This company was the precursor to today's Wall Street Journal, and both Dow and Jones are household words thanks to the industrial stock average that Dow first unveiled in May of 1896.

Millions of people in the U.S. receive information on the stock market every day from broadcast media. One of the first things that they will read or hear is the value of an index. The most popular stock index is the Dow Jones Industrial Average (DJIA). This index is so popular, that when many refer to the market being up or down, what they are actually referring to is the DJIA or "the Dow" as it's often called.

The DJIA is currently made up of 30 stocks. Current Dow Stocks as of July 1, 1998 are

Allied Signal	Hewlett-Packard
Aluminum Company of America	IBM
American Express	International Paper
AT&T	Johnson & Johnson
Boeing	McDonald's
Caterpillar	Merck & Company
Chevron	3M
Coca-Cola	J.P. Morgan
Disney	Philip Morris
DuPont	Procter & Gamble
Eastman Kodak	Sears
Exxon	Travelers Group
General Electric	Union Carbide
General Motors	United Technology
Goodyear Tire	Wal-Mart Stores

In 1896, when Charles Dow invented the DJIA it was very easy to calculate. The prices of the 12 stocks that Dow had originally selected were added up and divided by 12. This method of producing an index is price-weighted. Stocks with higher prices will affect the index more than stocks with lower prices. For example, say stock A was trading at $50 per share and stock B was trading at $100 dollars per share. If each stock dropped

10%, then Stock A would drop $5 and stock B would drop by $10. Stock B's decline would cause twice as much decline in the index as Stock A's decline.

The DJIA is still price-weighted today and the size of the companies included in the index does not affect how a change in the price of their stock affects the index. Many adjustments have been made to the divisor over the years. For example, the divisor is adjusted when stocks are replaced or split. To determine the current divisor, look in the *Wall Street Journal* on page C3. If the divisor is .2500 and one of the 30 Dow stocks goes up $2, the DJIA will go up 2/.2500 or 8 points. If the Dow, which is made up of 30 stocks, goes up 120 points and we wish to determine how much each stock went up on the average, we do so as follows: (120 points/30 stocks) x .2500 = 1. Thus, a 120 point change in the Dow represents a $1 change on the average in each of the Dow stocks. Remember to check the *Wall Street Journal* for the current Dow divisor, if you wish try some calculations. One criticism of a price-weighted index is that there is a bias toward higher priced stocks. A stock split does not affect the actual value of a stock. But when a stock splits, it becomes less influential in the index. There is no real economic justification for this. It is a characteristic of price-weighted indexes. When the stock splits, the divisor must be adjusted, otherwise the value of the index would change every time there was a stock split. An advantage of a price-weighted index is that it isn't very difficult to duplicate the return of the index. It only requires buying an equal number of shares of each of the stocks in the index.

All indexes have some weakness and have been criticized in various ways. The DJIA with its 30 industrial stocks might be not be considered broad enough. This criticism is probably less

valid today than historically, because some of the DJIA companies are actually giant conglomerates which themselves consist
of other diverse companies. For example, Disney owns an NHL
hockey team, a book publisher and hotels in addition to theme
parks. Another potential problem is that the DJIA gives a
higher weight to its high priced stocks, since the DJIA is price
weighted. A $100 per share stock that rises 2% will effect the
DJIA twice as much as a $50 that rises 2% per share.

STANDARD & POOR'S COMPOSITE 500

The Standard & Poor's Composite 500 (S&P 500) index
consists of 500 stocks. The stocks are selected based on market
capitalization, industry group representation and liquidity. If a
stock is removed then one is added to take its place. Stocks are
added or removed by the S&P 500 Index Committee. Removal
is usually for companies that have undergone a merger, acquisi-
tion, leveraged buyout, or bankruptcy. The committee may also
remove a company from the index after a restructuring. The
committee will review a company and any spin-offs after a restructuring to determine if it will remain in the index. The committee can also remove a company if it no longer feels that the
company is representative of its particular industry group. Some
guidelines for adding stocks to the index are based on market
value, industry group classification, capitalization, trading activity, operating condition and fundamental analysis.

Unlike the Dow, which is price-weighted, the S&P 500 is
value-weighted. A value-weighted index is based on market
capitalization. Market capitalization of a stock is the value of all
outstanding shares. Thus, a value-weighted index is based on
the value of all the outstanding shares not the price of a share. A

company's market capitalization does not change when a stock splits. If a company had 10,000,000 shares outstanding at a price of $50, its market capitalization is 10,000,000 x $50 or $500,000,000. If the stock splits two for one, then there are 20,000,000 shares outstanding at a price of $25, which equates to the same market capitalization of $500,000,000. No adjustments are required for stock splits in a value-weighted index. The greater the market capitalization of a stock the greater it will affect the index.

Another type of index is an equally-weighted index. To calculate this type of index, each stock is given an equal weight. Market capitalization or share price are ignored. For an investor to mimic this type of index, a portfolio would be created with an equal value of each stock. For example, it the index had ten stocks and the investor had $10,000 to invest, $1,000 would be invested in each stock.

More people than ever now own shares in mutual funds. Two possible reasons for this are a robust market and the popularity of 401k plans offered by employers. When employees enroll in 401k plans, they usually receive a selection of a number of different funds from which to select. Because employers often match employees' contributions either in whole or in part, it is advantageous for employees to participate in the plan. Some plans are structured so that employees who do not participate lose out on receiving matching contributions from the employer. Another incentive to participate are the income tax advantages. Income taxes are deferred on both the moneys invested and on the earnings of the investment. When employees are eligible to enroll, they often receive brochures describing the different selections. These usually contain a description of the fund, including performance for one, three, five and ten years, if the fund has been in existence for that long. There may also be a rating such as Morningstar's. Often there is a comparison of the fund's performance relative to an index. The selection of which index to use is of course made by the company offering the fund. It is interesting to note how many of the funds outperform the index that they are compared to. It can be interesting as well as enlightening to compare the fund's performance to additional indexes.

Indexes can be compared to those similar to the fund, such as comparing a global fund to a global index, or compared to a broad index such as the S&P 500 or Russell 2000. With so much information so readily available on the Internet, it is probably worth spending a little extra time comparing the fund's performance to indexes of your own choosing, rather than just relying on the information provided by the company selling the fund.

The age and number of miles on a car's odometer doesn't tell the whole story on a car's condition. However, just like an index, it can be a tool to give us concise and important information on which to base a buy, sell, or hold decision. So although indexes aren't perfect measurements of the stock market they can be a reasonable indication of market or sector performance. Given the current state of mass media they are easily available to investors.

CONSUMER PRICE INDEX

We have all heard stories about how one hundred dollars invested in IBM or AT&T many years ago would be worth vast sums today. We also know about nickel candy bars and workers working for ten dollars a day and being happy with the pay rate. How do we put this historical data in perspective? Inflation erodes returns, but how do we determine by how much? Does a worker in 1937 being paid ten dollars per day have more purchasing power than a worker in 1997 being paid $100 dollars a day? To determine the answer we must adjust for inflation. Without adjusting for inflation no investor can compare her real return for investments. The Consumer Price Index (CPI) is a tool that can be used to help adjust for inflation. But no tool is perfect, and it is believed by many that the CPI may overstate inflation somewhat.

The CPI is determined by the Bureau of Labor Statistics (BLS) and measures the prices paid by urban consumers for a predetermined list of goods and services. Each month the BLS gathers information from thousands of retail stores, service establishments, rental units and doctors' offices throughout the United States. The price movement in specific items is weighted according to its importance in population spending patterns. The combination of all factors then produces a weighted measurement of price change for the CPI. If the index changes during a period from 100 to 110, then it is reported that there has been a 10 percent increase in the CPI over the period. Each month the BLS reports thousands of detailed CPI numbers. Often the CPI number we hear most often announced in the press is the Consumer Price Index for All Urban Consumers (CPI-U).

Types of announcements that might be reported by the mass media about the CPI are the following:

1. The 12 month percentage change ending in March is 4.2 percent.

2. The annual rate of percent change so far this year if the rate for the first seven months continued for the full year would be 3.4 percent.

3. The one month seasonally adjusted basis for June was 0.2 percent.

The CPI can be used to compute the *real rate of return*, or inflation adjusted rate return, of an investment. The returns we have discussed thus far are *nominal rates of return*. These returns represent the percent change in dollars and do not consider changes in purchasing power. Suppose an investment of $10,000 had a return of 20% for one year. Also, assume the CPI increased by 5% over this same period. What is the real rate of return for this investment? The nominal return is 20% and the inflation rate is 5%, using the CPI as the measure of inflation. The naïve method to compute the real return is to take the difference: nominal rate - inflation rate = 20% - 5% = 15%. This is almost correct, and is usually a good approximation. Why is it not exact? The investment had a real return in dollars, after adjusting for inflation, of (15%) x ($10,000) = $1,500. But this is a return on an inflation-adjusted investment of (1+5%) x (10,000) = $10,500. Thus the real rate of return is $1,500/$10,500 = 14.3%, a little less than 15%. The general formula is

$$\text{real rate} = \frac{\text{nominal rate} - \text{inflation rate}}{1 + \text{inflation rate}}.$$

Simply taking the difference between the nominal and inflation rates will always result in a rate greater than the actual real rate (unless there is deflation). Using this formula to compute the real rate of return for our example we should get the same answer as before,

$$\text{real rate} = \frac{.20 - .05}{1 + .05} = .143 \text{ or } 14.3\%.$$

And now finally who is better off, the worker in 1937 earning ten dollars per day or the worker in 1997 earning \$100 per day? The CPI in December of 1937 was 14.4 and in 1997 it was 161.3. This represents an 11.2 fold increase. Thus, ten 1937 dollars would have the buying power of 112 dollars in 1997.

7

ADVANCED TOPICS

Everybody would like to better understand how the stock market and financial markets in general behave. The rewards for finding a better technique can be huge. Consequently, there is an enormous amount of research continually being published concerning these topics. This chapter will discuss two of these topics, the ARCH/GARCH models and neural networks. Developed recently, the ARCH models account for both a variable mean and a variable variance within a single equation that attempts to forecast stock returns. The more advanced and "generalized" models are the GARCH. These research instruments help their users predict movement of interest rates, exchange rates, and risky securities traded in efficient markets.

Within each of these topics, there is an enormous amount of literature. My objective is simply to introduce these techniques at a very basic level and to give the reader some feel for how they work. For those interested in pursuing these topics further, there are references listed in the supplemental bibliography.

MODELING VOLATILITY: THE ARCH/GARCH MODELS

As noted earlier, on October 18, 1987, Black Monday, the Dow Jones Industrial Average (DJIA) fell by 23%, the largest one day percent drop in history. In the following weeks the market had large swings. Suppose we followed the DJIA over a longer period of time. The following figure shows the monthly percent change in the DJIA from January 1990 to December 1995. Notice that large swings tend to be followed by more of the same, either up or down.

This phenomenon of high volatility followed by more high volatility is known as *volatility clustering*. It usually begins with a large shift in the market, which is then followed by large movements in either direction. The ARCH/GARCH provide an innovative method to model time series data which contain this volatility clustering property.

Time series data are observations taken at regularly spaced intervals, for example, the quarterly rate of return of IBM stock or the monthly percent change in the DJIA. Figure 7.1 is an example of time series data. The important characteristic that distinguishes this type of data from others is autocorrelation: when an observation is related to previous values of the same variable. For example, if this month's return for IBM stock is related to last month's return, then these returns are autocorrelated. Mathematical models which take advantage of autocorrelation are more appropriate than ones that do not. An-

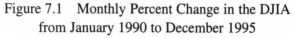

Figure 7.1   Monthly Percent Change in the DJIA
from January 1990 to December 1995

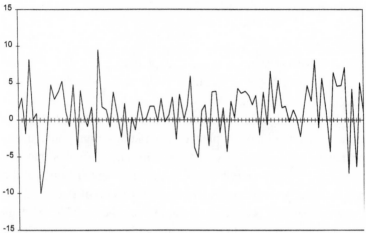

alysts have long had methods to develop these models, but most of these methods assumed a constant variance over time—which is sometimes unrealistic. Recall that we use the variance as a measure of volatility, so these models do not take into account any volatility clustering in the data. For this reason, ARCH/GARCH models can be particularly useful.

In 1982, Robert Engle introduced the AutoRegressive Conditional Heteroscedasticity (ARCH) process.[1] It allows the (conditional) variance to change over time as a function of past information. In statistical jargon, heteroscedasticity means unequal variance—or irregular volatility for financial data.

Our first step in describing the ARCH process is to define a

---

[1] Robert Engle, "Autoregressive Conditional Heteroscedasticity with Estimates of the Variance of United Kingdom Inflation," *Econometrica,* Vol. 50 (July, 1982), pp. 987–1007.

model for y_t, the value at time t of the variable of interest, such as a rate of return of a stock. Now consider the following regression equation for y_t:

$$y_t = c + b_1 x_1 + b_2 x_2 \ldots + e_t.$$

where c is a constant, x_i is the ith explanatory variable, b_i is the weight or coefficient of x_i, and e_t is the error term. The b_i's are estimated based on historical data.

This model implies that the return can be modeled as the sum of the weighted explanatory variables plus some unexpected noise. Explanatory variables are any variables that can be used to predict the return. Often they are lagged values of the return. A lagged variable is simply a past value of that variable. For example, if y_t is the current value, then the variable that lags by one period is y_{t-1}, which is last period's value. A lagged variable may go back several periods, as long as it has been determined to be useful in the model. The following is the simplest example of a model with a lagged variable. It is called a first-order autoregression.

$$y_t = c + b_1 y_{t-1} + e_t$$

It is important to distinguish between unconditional and conditional expectation. We will use the notation E_{t-1} which refers to the expectation conditional on the information set that can be used to predict y_t. This information set will usually contain lagged variables whose values are known at time $t - 1$. This notation is similar to Engle's work. Engle provides an excellent introduction to models for volatility. [2]

[2] Robert Engle, "Statistical Models for Financial Volatility," *Financial Analysts Journal*, (January–February, 1993) pp. 72–78.

Using the general regression model given earlier, we can write the equation for $E_{t-1}(y_t)$, the conditional expected value (or mean) of y_t as

$$E_{t-1}(y_t) = c + b_1 x_1 + b_2 x_2 + \dots$$

This is the same equation as for y_t except the error term drops out of the equation, since its expected value is assumed to be zero. Thus, this error term represents the difference between the actual realized return and its expected value, or

$$e_t = y_t - E_{t-1}(y_t).$$

The conditional variance of e_t and y_t are equal. Since $E_{t-1}(y_t)$ is a constant and adding or subtracting a constant does not affect the variance. Also, from the definition of the variance we can write the conditional variance of e_t as $E_{t-1}(e_t - 0)^2$ or $E_{t-1}(e_t)^2$, since the mean of e_t is zero. Further, $E_{t-1}(e_t)^2$ is equivalent to $E_{t-1}[y_t - E_{t-1}(y_t)]^2$ which is the conditional variance of y_t. This means that the error or noise is the component in the model which provides for the unexpected volatility in the variable we are modeling given the information set at $t - 1$.

Prior to ARCH, it was standard practice to assume that the distribution of e_t had constant variance, in addition to a mean of 0. This meant that uneven fluctuations in the market were not factored into the equation. But stock market data is likely to contain volatility clustering, and so we would expect the variance of the errors to vary over time. Thus, ARCH attempts to improve on the model by allowing for this form of heteroscedasticity. It specifies a conditional variance equation similar to the concept of the conditional mean equation. If we let h_t

equal the conditional variance of e_t, then one simple form of the ARCH model is given by

$$h_t = c + \alpha_1 e_{t-1}^2 + \alpha_2 e_{t-2}^2 + \ldots + \alpha_p e_{t-p}^2$$

This is an ARCH model of order p or ARCH(p). It can be viewed as a weighted sum (or average) of the previous p squared errors, where α_is are the weights. The squared errors are used since as we previously noted the conditional variance of e_t, h_t, can be written as $h_t = E_{t-1}(e_t)^2$. Thus, modeling the variance is equivalent to modeling the expected value of the squared error.

Notice that if we did assume constant variance, then we would likely want to make the weights α_i all equal to $1/p$, and c to be zero. This would reduce the ARCH model to simply computing the variance of the previous p errors. However, if we feel that the variance is changing over time then we would want the weights to reflect this fact. For example, we might observe that variances closer together in time are more correlated, as is the case in volatility clustering. If so, we would want to give more weight to recent squared errors and less weight to ones far in the past. The ARCH methodology uses historical data to estimate the "best" weights to predict future variance. The method generally used to obtain the weights is called maximum likelihood estimation. This procedure makes assumptions concerning the distribution of errors, usually that it is normal, and then finds the weights which maximize the likelihood of observing the historical data. The details of this procedure are far beyond the scope of this book and interested readers should see the previous cited references.

In 1986, Tim Bollerslev generalized the ARCH models to

obtain the Generalized AutoRegressive Conditional Heteroskedasticity (GARCH) models.[3] It allows for past conditional variances to be included in the model. One form is called the GARCH (p,q) and is given by

$$h_t = c + \alpha_1 e_{t-1}^2 + \alpha_2 e_{t-2}^2 + ... + \alpha_p e_{t-p}^2 + \beta_1 h_{t-1} + \beta_2 h_{t-2} + ... \beta_q h_{t-q}$$

Notice the addition of the last terms in the equation. They represent a weighted sum of past q variances where the β_i's are the weights. Again, maximum likelihood methodology can be used to estimate all the weights, along with the constant c. The option of different p and q's offers us a large class of models to choose from. But it has been found that in many cases the following GARCH $(1,1)$ is adequate.

$$h_t = c + \alpha_1 e_{t-1}^2 + \beta_1 h_{t-1}$$

The GARCH (p,q) model estimates the conditional variance based on a function which is linear in the past squared errors and variances. This means that the model does not make any distinction between negative and positive errors, that they have the same effect in the model. There are many alternative functional forms of this model. For example, it has been suggested that negative and positive swings in the market do not have the same effect on volatility. Thus, we might wish to use one of the alternative forms which does allow for different weights for different signs of the errors.

We have discussed how an asset with high risk or volatility should provide a higher mean return in order to attract risk-averse investors. In 1987, Engle, Lilien and Robins proposed a

[3] Tim Bollerslev, "Generalized Autoregressive Conditional Heteroskedasticity," *Journal of Econometrics*, Vol. 31 (1986), pp. 307–327.

model, called the ARCH-M (or GARCH-M), which incorporates the conditional variance into conditional mean equation.[4] This formulation allows for the utilization of the GARCH models to aid in the estimation of expected returns.

Accurately estimating variance is essential to investment theory. Many pricing models, such as the Black-Scholes, explicitly require an estimate of the variance. In 1963, Benoit Mandlebrot observed that "large changes tend to be followed by large changes—of either sign."[5] The ARCH and GARCH processes may provide an effective way to model this volatility over time.

NEURAL NETWORKS

"Artificial" neural networks are mathematical models that attempt to mimic the way the human brain processes information. As early as 1943, Warren McCulloch, a biologist, and Walter Pitts, a statistician, tried to model the brain's powerful ability to learn and organize information.[6] Researchers who develop neural networks attempt to imitate a key cell in the brain: the neuron. The brain contains billions of these neurons, which act as processing units that receive and combine signals from other neurons. These interconnected neurons form the basic concept of a network.

[4] Robert Engle, David Lilien, and Russell Robins, "Estimating Time Varying Risk Premia in the Term Structure: The ARCH-M Model," *Econometrica*, Vol. 55, (March, 1987), pp.391–407.

[5] Benoit Mandlebrot, "The Variation of Certain Speculative Prices," *Journal of Business*, 36, pp. 394–419.

[6] Warren McCulloch and Walter Pitts, " A Logical Calculus of Ideas Immanent in Nervous Activity, " *Bulletin of Mathematical Biophysics*, 5, pp. 115–133.

An artificial neural network contains nodes which play the role of the neurons. There are several layers of these nodes. The first layer is the input layer, where the information—be it the movements of a stock or those of the market as a whole—enters the network. Then, there may be one or more hidden layers which process the information, and finally an output layer which contains the results. Figure 7.2 displays what a simple neural network might look like.

Figure 7.2   A Simple Neural Network

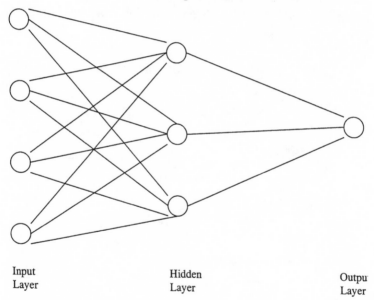

Input
Layer

Hidden
Layer

Outpu
Layer

This is an example of a network model with one hidden layer. Each circle represents a node. Notice that all the inputs feed into each node in the hidden layer. These inputs are given weights and then combined usually by summing. This sum is then mapped by a transfer function, which sends the signal to a node in the next layer or in this case the output node. This process is illustrated by the following figure.

Many times the transfer function is a threshold function which will pass information only if a certain level is reached. The network is trained by historical data, which is needed to determine the appropriate weights.

This discussion is only intended to give the reader a little of the flavor of neural networks. The details and the mathematics are extensive, and the interested reader should pursue further reading in any of the texts listed in the supplemental bibliography that are devoted to this subject.

Figure 7.3   A Processing Node

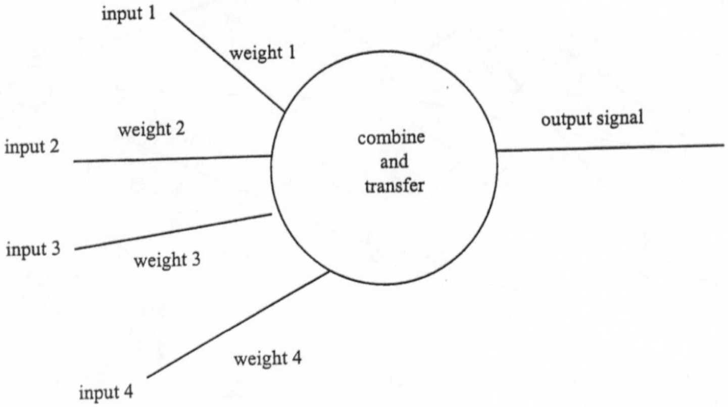

SELECTED BIBLIOGRAPHY

The following is a sample of some of the excellent textbooks which provide more detailed and complete coverage of many of the topics in this book. Of special note is material concerning modern portfolio theory, the capital asset pricing model, arbitrage pricing theory and performance measuring.

The books without the "*" do not assume the reader is familiar with advanced mathematics and an attempt has usually been made to use advanced mathematics only when necessary (although some knowledge of probability and statistics would be helpful). The books with the "*" are for the more mathematically adventurous, since they assume a higher level of mathematics.

Bodie, Zvi, Kane, Alex and Markus, Alan. *Investments*, Third Edition. New York: Irwin/Mcgraw-Hill, 1996.

* Campbell, John Y., Lo, Andrew W., MacKinlay, A. Craig., *The Econometrics of Financial Markets*. Princeton, New Jersey: Princeton University Press, 1997.

Jones, Charles P. *Investments, Analysis and Management*, Sixth Edition. New York: John Wiley & Sons, 1998.

Levy, Haim. *Introduction to Investments*. Cincinnati, Ohio: South Western College Publishing, 1996.

* Luenberger, David G., *Investment Science*, New York: Oxford University Press, 1998.

The following two books are devoted to artificial neural networks:

Hartz, John, et al. *Introduction to the Theory of Neural Computations*. Redwood City, CA: Addison-Wesley, 1991.

White, Halbert, *Artificial Neural Networks*. Cambridge, MA: Blackwell, 1992.